THE NEW BOUTIQUE

Neil Bingham

THE NEW BOUTIQUE
FASHION AND DESIGN

MERRELL

LONDON · NEW YORK

To my sister, Lynne (1942–2001),
who showed me how to love design

First published 2005 by Merrell Publishers Limited

Head office
42 Southwark Street
London SE1 1UN

New York office
49 West 24th Street, 8th floor
New York, NY 10010

www.merrellpublishers.com

Publisher: Hugh Merrell
Editorial Director: Julian Honer
US Director: Joan Brookbank
Sales and Marketing Director: Emilie Amos
Sales and Marketing Executive: Emily Sanders
Managing Editor: Anthea Snow
Editor: Sam Wythe
Design Manager: Nicola Bailey
Junior Designer: Paul Shinn
Production Manager: Michelle Draycott
Production Controller: Sadie Butler

British Library Cataloguing-in-Publication Data:
Bingham, Neil R.
The new boutique : fashion and design
1.Speciality stores – Design 2.Fashion merchandising
3.Speciality stores – Design – Pictorial works 4.Fashion
merchandising – Pictorial works
I.Title
725.2'1

ISBN 1 85894 257 8

Designed by Maggi Smith
Project managed by Marion Moisy
Copy-edited by Caroline Ball
Proof-read by Kim Richardson
Indexed by Hilary Bird

Printed and bound in China

FRONT JACKET Marni, London
BACK JACKET (left to right) Jil Sander, London; Gianfranco Ferré,
Milan; Alexander McQueen, New York; Jean Paul Gaultier, Paris;
Prada Epicenter, Tokyo
PAGE 2 Issey Miyake Tribeca, New York

CONTENTS

INTRODUCTION

Dolce & Gabbana, Milan: The designers' flagship store is in an eighteenth-century palazzo restored by David Chipperfield, with interior design by Ferruccio Laviani.

The true royalty of fashion boutiques reign in the world's fashion capitals: London, Milan, New York, Paris and Tokyo. By tradition, these luxury shops are where handsome dark-suited men, the boutique bouncers, open the door for you with a cool but knowing smile. Highly professional staff of smartly dressed women and moonlighting male models tip you a quiet welcoming word. The air is subtly filled with music, fragrant with scent. Beautiful clothes are attractively displayed in a dazzling setting. You don't even have to look at the price tag of that little dress – if there is a price tag – because it is probably the same as a round-the-world airline ticket, first class. The experience is intoxicating, empowering.

This is boutique seduction, by fashion and design.

The retailing of luxury and unique clothing has carried on, in much simpler forms, for hundreds of years. It is just that since the end of the Second World War, as the Western economy grew richer, exclusive little retail shops became more widespread, reaching a broader audience. By the late 1990s, the cult of the fashion designer and fashion labels had developed into a global phenomenon (that is, if you live in a prosperous area of the globe). So by the early years of the twenty-first century – when all the boutiques discussed and illustrated in this book first

Prada Epicenter, New York: Electronic screens hang from the clothing rails, displaying product information, videos and graphic images.

opened their doors – the competitive retailing of clothing at the high end of the market had created larger and more innovative showcases for display. The boundaries between retail and art and architecture blurred as an increasing number of architects and artists of exceptional talent and international reputation worked with fashion designers, reshaping the world of fashion architecture. Fashion and design had collided in an explosive fusion – the new boutique.

Each fashion designer, each fashion house, has a style. This is what architects attempt to interpret through boutique design. "You must have an understanding of the designer's ideas," observes Michael Gabellini, one of the most prominent architects in the field, "or at least a leap of faith," he adds with amusement.[1] The search is for visual metaphor or, more commercially put, branding image, to make clear, or at least subtly transparent, the designer's ethos. Already the fashion designer

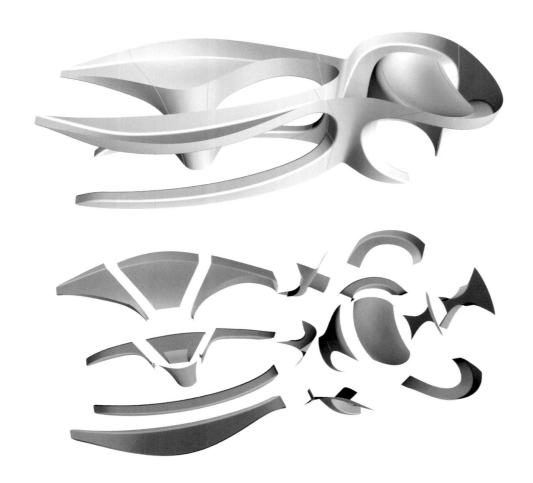

Carlos Miele, New York: The computer-generated exploded image of the sculpted interior, created by the boutique's architects Asymptote, illustrates the component parts of the structure.

and the architect have a language in common: the fabric of a suit/the fabric of a building, the structure, construction, model, materials, finishings, pattern, decoration …[2]

The high-design experience of the exquisitely architect-designed boutique is the principal theme of today's top fashion boutiques and, like the clientele, comes in many shapes and sizes. Some hot fashion designers are still finding their boutique feet. The great designer John Galliano, who since 1996 has been head of the House of Dior, opened his first own-label boutique in Paris only in 2003, designed by the architect Jean-Michel Wilmotte. Carlos Miele, with sixty boutiques in his native Brazil, finally triumphed in New York with a boutique in the meatpacking district on lower Manhattan – the whiffiest but trendiest fashion area; the liquid-like computer-generated boutique interior was created by the architectural team at Asymptote. At the other end of the scale, the large fashion house Prada, which maintains an instantly recognizable global network of boutiques with standard mint-green interiors, has played high stakes by commissioning celebrity architects such as Rem Koolhaas and Herzog & de Meuron to create large, attention-grabbing, one-off experimental boutiques in Los Angeles, New York and Tokyo.

Maison Martin Margiela, London: A publicity shot for the opening of the London boutique references the fashion house's white-out style.

Some major fashion boutiques don't have architects. Well, they do, but the poor things work quietly and anonymously behind the dressing room curtain, carrying out the instructions of the fashion designer client. An example is the Belgian designer Martin Margiela, who calls himself Maison Martin Margiela, implying that his whole fashion house is one identity. He has all his boutiques painted white, including the flea-market furniture. It goes with his style of anonymity, which might seem

Celux, Tokyo: The private members' boutique, designed by Tim Power.

simplistic, but in its understatement is skilfully sophisticated and exclusive. When you walk into one of his boutiques, you either get it or you don't … and if you don't, you're a fashion washout.

Fashion designers, fashion houses and big fashion conglomerates are out to create not only an identifiable image for their boutiques, but also one that rides the crest of the next design wave. For all the glamour, this is the big business of marketing, of keeping investors happy. And it's a harsh world out there, where many a hand-stitched suit gets slashed to ribbons in the fight to stay ahead. "We show in order to sell", bluntly reads the opening line of Martin Pegler's classic textbook on shop display, which is on the bookshelf of every boutique architect.[3] There is a constant striving for new ways to entice clients back, and give them new experiences. The Louis Vuitton club in Tokyo, called Celux, is but one example of pushing the boutique boundaries: here clients, in the privacy of their exclusive and beautifully designed club by Tim Power, can sip champagne and look at select fashion items. This is the world of Nu-Lux, new luxury.

One of the greatest novelties in the past few years has been the publicity surrounding the opening of many of the new boutiques, with enormous razzmatazz in the fashion press, as well as in the architectural and design press and, most interestingly – and necessary for continued global business – in the public press and popular media. Boutiques are part of the mass interest in designer celebrity and in the famous people who shop in these luxury boutiques. The designer

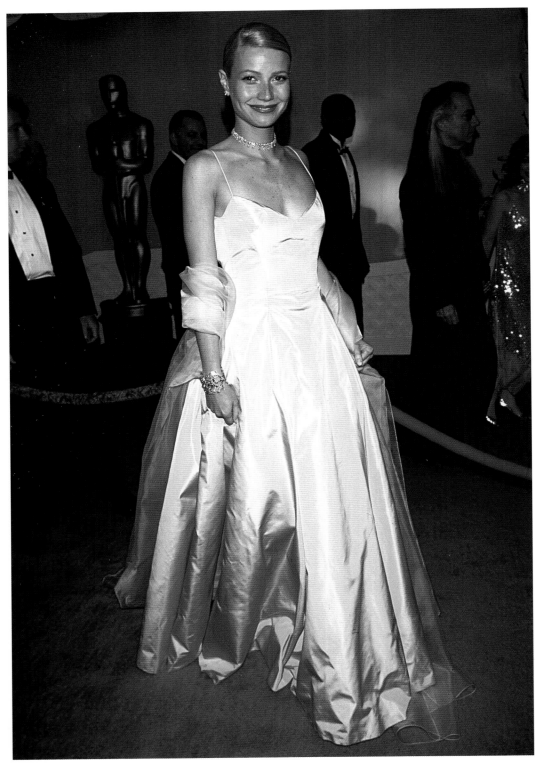

Gwyneth Paltrow wearing Ralph Lauren on the red carpet at the Academy Awards ceremony in 1999. Celebrity events have made haute couture an essential part of popular culture.

dress that makes Gwyneth Paltrow even more ravishing as she strikes a red-carpet pose on Academy Awards night is shown around the world as a live television event, and is the next day's front page splash and big Internet hit. That moment makes and retains fashion designers as superstars, and entices more customers across the threshold of the new boutique.

It's all a matter of association, and it washes through the new boutique on to the architect. And this is certainly part of new boutique practice: famous architects are hanging around with famous fashion designers. Not that they didn't a hundred years ago, but it was then a very small world known only to the cognoscenti; there was no mass media interest or hype.

Perhaps this book is but another example of a need to indulge in aspirations, both yours and mine, to touch somehow that fascinating world that these boutiques inhabit between fact and fiction, fantasy and desire. Whatever the motive, I hope that this book manages to impart some of their excitement and beauty, to illustrate the most innovative designs, and illuminate the historical and visual links between fashion and design that make the new boutique.

Is Nothing New?

Scratch a new boutique (although it's not to be recommended when the boutique bouncers are watching) and beneath you will find many old ideas. Historically, the new boutique has developed out of two related fashion strands: the private apartments of the couturier, and pretty little luxury shops. In the nineteenth century, couturiers dressed European aristocrats and wealthy Americans, visiting clients in their homes. However, when the Englishman Charles Worth (1825–1895) set up his own *maison de couture* in Paris in 1858, his clients came to him. *Maisons de couture* became established in those areas of retail wealth where the most prestigious sections of the fashion industry still cluster today. For example, in London in the 1890s Lucille was in Old Burlington Street, the little street where Jil Sander currently has her grand boutique. Lucille subsequently moved to Hanover Square, home today of British *Vogue* magazine, just off New Bond Street, the most concentrated avenue of London's fashion parade of boutiques. In New York, Mariano Fortuny established in 1929 on Madison Avenue, today a canyon of designer boutiques. Each of these *maisons* featured fine rooms to complement the clothing. There was the "Rose Room", with walls and daybed hung with pale-pink taffeta and lace, and the boudoir for intimate apparel.[4]

Paris was the velvet setting for the *beau monde* in the late nineteenth and early twentieth centuries, the city a backdrop of the small luxury shop – *la boutique* – for hats, flowers, jewellery, gloves, books, clothing, decorative objects. At the *fin de siècle*, with Art Nouveau in full flourish, the boutique façade enjoyed a highly ornamental prosperity; the interiors were of equal lushness, although by today's standards they seem statically planned. All the exteriors and many of the fittings of these boutiques were architect-designed.[5]

Early twentieth-century Modernism brought a mixed reaction by architects to designing

Publications on architect-designed boutiques began to be produced in the early twentieth century. Two of the most influential were *Boutiques 1931* (below left), a compendium of fashionable French Art Deco boutiques written by Roger Poulain, and L.P. Sézille's *Devantures de boutiques* (1927), which featured a 1920s design by Pierre Chareau for a Parisian decorator's boutique (below right).

fashion shops. Architects have tended to inhabit a highly moralistic universe, and the founders of the Modernist movement in particular were prone to pontificating upon the ethical rights and wrongs within design. Although leading architects such as Peter Behrens, Josef Hoffmann, Henri van de Velde, Otto Wagner and Frank Lloyd Wright designed dresses for their wives, for most of them fashion was superficial, ephemeral and effeminate.[6] Architecture, unlike the cut of a waistcoat or evening gown, was not a passing fashion, it was eternal. And those boutiques were nothing but little bonbons.

Nevertheless, the 1920s and early 1930s was a golden period, when Modernism and boutique culture nurtured innovative and stylish designs that resonate still in the new boutique of today. Paris wore the crown as the queen of fashion and of the boutique, but in those cities where Modernism was emerging – particularly in Berlin, Stuttgart, Rotterdam, Prague and New York – boutique design was carried delightfully in its wake. In this period, exquisitely illustrated publications on architect-designed boutiques began to appear, mainly in France, written by architects. There was Sézille's *Devantures de boutiques* of 1927, with hand-coloured plates showing built projects alongside design drawings.[7] And, with fine interior photographs and a striking cover, Roger Poulain's *Boutiques 1931*.[8] In one of his several books on the subject, René Herbst trumpeted: *"Le décor des boutiques et magasins est actuellement en pleine évolution"*– the decoration of boutiques and stores is at present constantly evolving.[9] Boutiques became sleek, inside and out; colour was used with a broad brush; metals such as steel and aluminium were favoured; and glass was everywhere, from the expansive show window to display tabletops. Illumination and lighting became an important technique for highlighting façades and display.[10]

The Pellicceria Zanini boutique, Milan, 1950 (below left) and Jil Sander, London, 2002 (below right). Although more than fifty years separate these two boutiques, each uses ceiling-suspended display units.

French Dressing, off Carnaby Street, London, late 1960s: A colourful graphic of a hallucinogenic mushroom was painted on to the boutique façade, reflecting the Pop era's new, hip combination of drugs and fashion.

During the Depression of the 1930s, and the ensuing Second World War, boutique design in America slowed, while in Europe it slowed then ceased. In the late 1940s, Paris revived its reputation as the centre of chic with Christian Dior's head-turning New Look collection for spring 1947. Also in Paris at this time, the appellation 'boutique' became more closely associated with fashion when many of the *maisons de couture* opened boutiques selling *prêt-à-porter*, ready-to-wear clothing: simpler, usually machine-sewn versions of their couture collection. The couturiers referred to these lines as *confection*, an indication that they didn't take these garments, or probably their boutiques, too seriously. There were only a few of these boutiques in the 1930s, but after the war many of the large fashion houses found it convenient and profitable to have a boutique on the ground floor of their *maison*.

In post-war fashion centres such as Paris, Milan and Rome, and especially in America, where the economy was booming, the design of retail shops adopted the new Modernism based on attenuated and organic shapes, abstract pattern and lightweight materials.[11] Many well-known architects and designers turned their hands to boutique design: in New York among the new kids on the best blocks were Morris Lapidus, Raymond Loewy, Skidmore Owings & Merrill, and Harrison & Abramovitz.[12]

The Christa Metek boutique, Vienna, 1967: Exterior and interior views of the influential high-style boutique designed by architect Hans Hollein. With its plastic moulded fittings, this was Pop architecture at its most sophisticated.

Britain suffered great hardship after the war, and it was not until the 1960s that it once more took to the world stage. And when it did, London went all groovy. Swinging London. Pop, Rockers, Mods. The King's Road, Portobello Road, Carnaby Street – hang-outs synonymous with the boutique. The word 'boutique' entered the English language. I Was Lord Kitchener's Valet, Granny Takes a Trip, Biba, Bus Stop, Stop the Shop, I Spy – the alternative boutiques of acid-dropping psychedelic mini-skirts and second-hand uniforms to make you an honorary member of Sergeant Pepper's Lonely Hearts Club Band. Painted in large flower-power murals in Day-Glo colours and lit by black lights, the 1960s boutique loosened all past design principles, everything was left to all hang out.[13]

But even among this counter-culture was the steadying T-square of the architect and professional designer. Hans Hollein, future winner of the Pritzker Prize for Architecture, designed the Christa Metek boutique in Vienna with a cut-out circular façade in 1967. Terence Conran, the most successful British designer as well as restaurateur of the late twentieth century, created Mary Quant's Bazaar in London's Knightsbridge back in 1957. Polished stainless steel, perspex, plastics and fibreglass were the new materials, which could be moulded in a continuous surface. In Japan, a rising star in the boutique firmament as the Japanese economy boomed and things Western became hip, the gifted designer Shiro Kuramata used fibreglass to create cohesive boutiques such as Market One and Shop One in Tokyo in 1970. The shopfront and walls and ceilings merged in a single white skin, precursors of today's new boutiques by Asymptote for Carlos Miele or William Russell for Alexander McQueen.[14]

In the late 1960s, many of the designers who were to stitch their way to internationalism opened their first boutiques: Ralph Lauren, Jil Sander, Oscar de la Renta, Emanuel Ungaro, Rei Kawakubo with her Comme des Garçons. But it was Yves Saint Laurent opening his Rive Gauche

Yves Saint Laurent on the opening day of his boutique in Paris's Rive Gauche, 26 September 1966.

boutique in Paris's rue de Tournon in September 1966 that illustrated the revolution taking place at the high end of fashion boutiques. For here was a famous young couturier, no longer connected to a large *maison de couture*, selling a true *prêt-à-porter* collection in his own stand-alone boutique. Saint Laurent displayed his Pop-art dresses in a setting he had designed with the decorator Isabelle Hebey: red lacquered walls, bright orange rugs, space-age furniture by Olivier Morgue and colourful sculptures by Nikki de Saint-Phalle.[15] Soon other couturiers were opening their own ready-to-wear boutiques.

By the mid-1970s, boutique culture took a noticeable shift. Just as bell bottoms widened to their flappiest flare, the Western economy was slowed by an energy crisis brought on by Arab restrictions on oil exports. The world, including that of fashion, sobered up, and sophisticated up. The strong voices of architects and designers with international reputations were about to be heard in boutique design.

Throughout the 1980s and 1990s, there was a diversity of boutique styles, reflective of the multi-layered approach of the period. Out of the radicalism of the previous decades came the Italian architect and designer Ettore Sottsass, creating boutiques for Fiorucci and,

Joseph boutique, Sloane Street, London (opposite):
The glass-tread and steel-cable staircase by Eva Jiricna
(1989) was one of the first high-tech interiors of the
period. Katharine Hamnett boutique, London (above):
This expansive boutique, set in a converted garage
and designed by Norman Foster in 1987, was unique at
the time in not having a shop window and for allowing
the designer's collection a vast space to breathe.

under its inspirational founder Doug Tomkins, for Esprit.[16] These were Memphis interiors, the movement that Sottsass founded in 1981. Walls were of raw concrete, furniture and display units were chunky and covered in bright patterned laminates. The design team at Coop Himmelblau 'deconstructed' boutiques in their native Vienna and in Tokyo, by means of slender metal columns and flying footbridges.[17]

Of particular significance were a set of boutiques in London that had considerable influence on subsequent designs; their inspiration still resonates in the new boutique of today. Joseph Ettedgui was among the leaders of fashion designers to use the high-tech look for his boutiques. His architect was Eva Jiricna, whose interiors clinically clanked with stainless steel and glass. The staircase for the Joseph boutique on Sloane Street, from 1989, was constructed of glass treads set in polished pistons leading to techy heaven.[18] Jiricna's designs and construction set new standards of detailed architectural craftsmanship.

Norman Foster, too, had designed a boutique for Joseph, in 1978. But Foster's boutique for Katharine Hamnett, in 1987, shook up all previous concepts on boutique design. Set in a large former car repair workshop in the Brompton Road, near Conran's resurrection of the Michelin Building, the boutique was unique in not being set directly on the street. It had no shop window, just a wee sign. Entrance from the street was via an arched bridge of etched glass – a catwalk. The space, like a giant dance studio, was bare, white, naturally lit, with clothes hung on racks to one side, and the main feature was a white grand piano.[19] There was space everywhere; the collection breathed.

This paring down of the boutique interior developed in the late 1980s, coming to celebrated fruition in a style that is a principal movement within today's new boutique – minimalism. If not the first example, the most prominently noticeable, and setting a defining moment for minimalism, came with John Pawson's Calvin Klein boutique on Madison Avenue, New York, which opened in 1995. This British architect introduced Americans to a rich purity in materials, detailing and space. Enclosed by great sheets of windows, the boutique feels as if a razor-sharp knife has cut through its warm buttery interior: the floors are of the pale yellow stone from Pawson's native Yorkshire, the expansive walls are plain and white, display tables are dark slabs. And discreetly tucked into wall pockets is the collection of Calvin Klein's own minimal-style clothing.[20] Pawson's new boutique for Calvin Klein in Paris is its little sister.

New Collaborations

Remember when small was beautiful? Well, it still is, but so is big. The most noticeable trend of the new boutique is size: numerical and physical. The new boutiques are bigger, and everywhere. Louis Vuitton has three hundred boutiques in fifty countries and employs 9500 people; the Louis Vuitton boutique in Tokyo, by architect Jun Aoki, is nine storeys tall. There are more than a hundred Prada boutiques worldwide; in New York, the Prada Epicenter covers over 2000 sq. m (23,000 sq. ft). What happened to the innocence of the boutique, that small and intimate space? "If you lose the word 'boutique'," muses Peter Marino, the architect of the twenty-two-storey (or eleven double-height floors) Tokyo Chanel, "you lose luxury. Then it becomes a department store."[21]

It all began to change in the late 1980s. Elitist aspirations percolated between street culture and haute couture. The cult of the fashion designer moved into high gear. Everyone was wearing jackets jeans and T-shirts, and boasting accessories and handbags, emblazoned with the names of big fashion designers, all effortlessly acquired through outlets at the countless new malls. But there was a problem: it had a designer label, yet most probably the designer had nothing to do with it. And it showed. This was mass production, manufactured out-of-house under fashion licensing. Suddenly the sheen and mystique of many older fashion houses and designers – Yves Saint Laurent, Christian Dior, Pierre Cardin – dimmed, while the new designers, such as Giorgio Armani and Calvin Klein, who avoided bleeding their brand, were going from strength to strength.

Calvin Klein, Madison Avenue, New York, 1995: Classic minimalism by British architect John Pawson.

Large fashion houses began to smarten up their act. There were takeovers and radical makeovers. The fashion conglomerate was born, owning multi-labels, dealing with billions of dollars' worth of investments. The biggest player in the fashion game to emerge has been LVMH Moët Hennessy Louis Vuitton, under the direction of Bernard Arnault. Today, LVMH is the world's largest purveyor of luxury goods, from champagne to watches, owning department stores like the venerable La Samaritaine in Paris, and over a dozen of the big fashion houses. Arnault brought in hot young designers to regenerate faded fashion houses. In 1996 he appointed the whimsically wild John Galliano to design for Givenchy, moving him to Dior the following year. Bad boy Alexander McQueen came in at Givenchy. Hedi Slimane rejuvenated Dior Homme. It all proved immensely successful for design, and lucrative for the company.

Another large fashion conglomerate to develop in the 1990s was the Gucci Group. In 1994, the 32-year-old fashion designer Tom Ford became the group's creative director. Over the following ten years, Ford lifted the house of Gucci out of its decline and clichéd appearance, then went on to re-stimulate Yves Saint Laurent Rive Gauche, gathering the fledgling Stella McCartney under his wing.

The third large fashion group of the new period, Prada, is not on the hefty financial scale of LVMH or Gucci, but is nevertheless profitable (with its ups and downs) and sports a high profile and innovative concepts. The designer is Miuccia Prada, granddaughter of the company's founder, but the powerhouse behind the label is her husband, Patrizio Bertelli, the chief executive of the privately owned Prada Group. In a couple of his buying sprees he nabbed Helmut Lang and Jil Sander, putting them, it is rumoured, in the not very comfortable Pucci stable.

In the late 1990s, press and publicity crackled with these new market leaders. High fashion was front page news, be it a takeover bid or the appearance of that perfect fashion model, Diana, Princess of Wales at a royal function wearing a new designer outfit. Pop songs and television programmes revelled in labels. "It's a Lacroix, sweetie," always slurred Eddy (the comedian actress Jennifer Saunders) in the TV hit *Absolutely Fabulous* when asked what she was wearing.

Entering the new millennium, the fashion world found itself transformed. It had become a true industry, predominantly market led, not as in the old days when couturiers ruled and their clients ogled and followed.[22] Whereas once a successful designer or fashion house had only a boutique or two in each of the major world cities and resorts, now outlets sprang up seemingly around every corner: in airports, in the new rich markets in the Middle East, and in fashion-fixated Japan. Fashion in Asia is a huge growth market.

With so many boutiques lining the pavements, how could each fashion house retain a personal aura, one strongly recognizable by a public bombarded by media messaging? Like any other big corporation, such as Coca-Cola or McDonald's, they meticulously developed their branding image. The new boutique became the jewel in the fashion-house crown. The world's five major fashion cities – London, Milan, New York, Paris and Tokyo – became home to the biggest and the brightest: the new mega-boutique, the flagship, the embassy, the epicentre.

Architects are no longer reticent about their alliance with the corporate world of fashion. They have come out of the closet and on to the streets. A hundred years ago, architects such as McKim Mead & White and Darling & Pearson lined the avenues of the great cities of North America (and many of the dusty roads of aspiring little prairie towns) with impressive Neo-classical bank buildings. These were the temples of corporate power. Today, it is the new boutique, representing the corporate clout of luxury shopping. The boutique has arrived; it's already part of a historic tradition, like the banking temple once was, in a continuity of past architectural symbols of authority – the cathedral and church, the royal palace, the country house of the landed gentry. Any stigma that may have been attached to designing boutiques has now disappeared as the ability to brand a product globally is recognized as an art in itself.

Marni boutique, Villa Moda shopping mall, Kuwait City, designed by Future Systems. The designer boutique is now a global phenomenon.

Many architects involved with the new boutique have emerged as leaders in the field of corporate retail practices in the luxury market. Particularly influential are Michael Gabellini, who has created boutiques for Jil Sander, Salvatore Ferragamo, Gianfranco Ferré and Giorgio Armani; Richard Gluckman for Gianni Versace and Helmut Lang; Peter Marino for Louis Vuitton and Chanel; John Pawson for Calvin Klein; and Claudio Silvestrin for Giorgio Armani. A very prominent architect theorizing and writing on retail is Rem Koolhaas, architect of the Prada Epicenter boutiques on Broadway in New York and on Rodeo Drive, Los Angeles. He and his two firms, OMA and AMO, have carried out dozens upon dozens of exploratory exercises for Prada. In 2001, he and his students published the 800-page *Harvard Design School guide to shopping*: a statistical, historical, illustrative, illuminating, playful study on consumer desire and brand survival.[23] Concurrently, Koolhaas produced a book on

Dolce & Gabbana headquarters, Milan, designed by
+ARCH, a firm also responsible for many of Dolce &
Gabbana boutiques. Such architects often design the
offices and showrooms for the big fashion houses.

This map from Rem Koolhaas's book *Projects for Prada*
(2001) illustrates the intense concentration of boutiques
in New York's SoHo district.

his partnership with Prada.[24] And again Prada, that leader in pushing retail boundaries, collaborated with the architects of their next boutique in Tokyo, Herzog & de Meuron, in publishing a book of fuzzy pictures and choppy statements specifically on that single project.[25] The new boutique had acquired a trendy intellectual cutting edge.

The sceptical opinion is that today's collaboration of architects with fashion and fashion powerhouses is nothing but a travesty, a commercial sell-out, the brainwashing of branding. This, you will find, is usually the view of Modernists who, perhaps admirably, quote Le Corbusier and equate architecture with eternal truths and ideals. Fashion is the new dictator in the arts, runs the argument, sponging off the high credentials of architecture. "The architect allows his work to be used as propaganda," taunts one critic.[26]

The more optimistic and widely held view is that fashion and architecture have always had much in common. Both fashion designer and architect explore similar territories: the sheltering of the body, the use of materials, aesthetics, the concepts of form and space.[27] The new boutique has become the ideal meeting place to explore these shared preoccupations.

No closer link exists than when the fashion designer is a qualified architect, or *vice versa*. Gianfranco Ferré, who in collaboration with Gabellini Associates designs his own principal boutiques, says of the fusion of his fashion and architectural values:

> I find that architecture is basically a discipline that is poised delicately between creative flair and method, between invention and logic. And this also corresponds perfectly to my way of 'sensing' fashion. Which for me is based on a profound concern with forms and how to elaborate them; it's an authentic construction process, a rational operation, similar to what occurs in architecture where one must deal with a spatial context in which a new building is to be located. Clothing, my clothing, at least, is textile architecture that has been designed for the human body, which brings the garments to life.[28]

Gianfranco Ferré, shown below on the catwalk after one of his shows, is unique in being both a fashion designer and a qualified architect; he is intimately involved in the design of his boutiques, such as one in via Sant'Andrea, Milan (below right).

Gianfranco Ferré's new boutique is like his 'textile architecture': luxurious, sumptuous and colourful, in a rich variety of materials. "The architecture and interior design of my new boutiques," Ferré concludes, "display a marked penchant for sophistication and versatility, the very same characteristics that have always distinguished my collections."[29]

As architect and fashion designer, Ferré does not have to go in search of the architectural metaphor for his fashion style. It is innate. But for every other architect and designer of the new boutique, finding and capturing the ethos of the fashion designer or fashion house is a requirement, not simply to get the branding right but in order to display the collection of garments to its greatest advantage. Such visual stimulus within boutique design induces customers into a silent dialogue with the fashion designer's broader vision. Usually, the more successfully the architect gets under the designer's petticoats, the more exciting the boutique design.

Making reference to fashion materials and tools of the trade is one technique used by architects and boutique designers to trigger the omnipresence of the fashion designer. Jun Aoki created the Louis Vuitton boutique in the Omotesando district of Tokyo in the image of a pile of travelling trunks stacked at random – the House of Louis Vuitton is historically famous for its trunks – and then covered the building in layers of metal meshing to form an optical moiré effect, as if two thin silks had been overlaid. Inside, the architects Eric Carlson and David McNulty hung great panels of stainless steel 'fabric' to simulate the fabric lining of a trunk.[30]

The walls of the Jean Paul Gaultier boutiques by Philippe Starck are textured in square padded taffeta panels inset with buttons, the technique known as *capitonné* that Gaultier sometimes integrates into his flamboyant fashions. The seven-storey Dior boutique by the architects SANAA in Tokyo's Omotesando district is wrapped in an acrylic thermoformed lining resembling dress fabric. Sophie Hicks, the architect for Paul Smith's Milan boutique, points out that her design for the terrazzo floor, with its coral pink edging delineating the new from the original sections, is "like patched jeans where you don't hide the mending".[31] Sean Dix, the designer for Moschino in via Sant'Andrea, Milan, laser-cut a wall and then backlit it to resemble lace, piled mounds of fabric to create a column, and stuck millions of pins in another column for decoration. "I used the materials associated with the construction of clothing as building elements," Dix comments.[32]

Architectural references to the fashion designer's style can be subtle. The twisting sculpture *Tornado*, by Frank Gehry, which whips its way through the Issey Miyake boutique in New York's Tribeca area, suggests Miyake's distinction for creating clothes of novel contour, flowing pleated line and movement. A Stella McCartney boutique by Universal Design Studio is about nature and the natural; McCartney, being a strong supporter of the countryside and animal welfare, uses no leathers, and her clothing style shows off the natural figure of the woman. A calm mysticism permeating through a total lifestyle is expected in the Donna Karan New York boutique, with its rich earthy colours, Zen-like rock garden and pool and indigenous artefacts, the perfect counterpoint to the designer's serene collection. Marcel Wanders has created a giant figure of Gulliver in the centre of the London Mandarina Duck boutique, the ultimate representation of the traveller who might well carry one of Mandarina Duck's famous pieces of luggage.

For the new boutique in Japan, architects often like to create the illusion that their building has been wrapped – *tsutsumu* – or has a tying or binding – *musubu* – which has the special meaning in Japanese beliefs and rituals of demarcating an object or space as special or sacred. SANAA's Dior is 'wrapped' in an acrylic fabric. Herzog & de Meuron's Prada building is 'tied' with strings of steel. Tim Power has a walnut 'wrapping' around the interior of the Celux boutique club.

For those fashion houses where the couturier has taken the final catwalk call, the architect usually evokes the ghost of the designer's style, reinforcing tradition in a contemporary manner. There is a great deal of humour and wit in Dix's Moschino boutiques, in deference to the irreverent attitude of the late founder of the house, Franco Moschino. For Chanel, Peter Marino alights on the late Coco's love of a black-and-white palette and on her taste in framing objects.

Some references are direct. The architects at Studio 63 play upon and exaggerate the modern retro look of the collection in the Miss Sixty boutiques, heaping shag pile carpets alongside psychedelic furniture. Dolce & Gabbana, the baroque queens of modern fashion, embellish many of their boutiques with 'his-and-his' thrones.

Undoubtedly the minimalist message is the hushed voice speaking loudest in the new boutique. The reduction of decoration resonates with so many of the collections by modern fashion designers: Pawson for Calvin Klein, Claudio Silvestrin and Michael Gabellini for Armani, Gluckman Mayner for Helmut Lang. And, moving one step beyond, edging into the twilight, is the invisible look. Maison Martin Margiela coats the whole interior of its boutiques in white, furniture and fixtures alike. Even the signboard outside is whitewashed over. But at least the London and Paris boutiques *have* shop windows, if not much in them. A little sign simply pointing down a Parisian alleyway is the only indication of the Comme des Garçons boutique, where the windows are blocked out. And only the true fashionistas know how to gain entrance to the very select collections at Paris's L'Eclaireur boutique, knowing which little doorbell to ring from a choice of so many buzzers and so many doors in rue Hérold.[33]

Although many boutiques are designed on a comfortable but limited budget, and unmistakably still find ways of speaking in unity with the designer's persona, the great global luxury boutiques seem to spare no expense in articulating the fashion programme. In the corporate boutiques, rich materials are applied as lavishly as beads and pearl drops are to a Galliano gown. Luxurious leathers and silks are essential accessories. Gold leaf, amber, semi-precious stones – onyx, lapis lazuli – seem to have been lifted out of a tale from the Arabian Nights. Architectural marbles and great slabs of stone are heaved halfway round the world, rare woods dragged from the Brazilian jungle, crystal cut as if by diamond specialists, great glass chandeliers hand-blown by the artisans on the Venetian island of Murano. The intensity of the luxury of the new boutique extends to the cutting edge of modern design: bespoke furniture from international designers, expensively tinted plexiglas partitions and perspex handrails, enveloping walls of perfectly engineered seamless stainless steel. The audacious use of opulent materials and the skills used can make an old sultan's palace look as everyday as a Wal-Mart. But this being Nu-Lux, the impression is discreet, private, downplayed, minimal, almost

Mandarina Duck, London: Preliminary design by Marcel Wanders. The giant figure of 'Gulliver' surveys the Lilliputian mannequins.

Prada Epicenter, Broadway, New York: Rem Koolhaas designed a 'hanging city' of moveable display cages suspended from motorized tracks.

imperceptible … to be felt in the touch, in the texture, with the knowledge that the materials are fine, craftsman-cut and finished, in the manner you experience and appreciate wearing a designer garment.

But luxury is not always enough to retain the attention of the fashion client who expects novelty and the unique. Just as the designer creates seasonal collections, so too must the new boutique continually reinvent itself. Some fashion designers deliberately limit the lifespan of their boutiques. The Issey Miyake Fete in Tokyo's Minami-Aoyama district had the most spectacular interior by the artist Kenji Yanobe for less than two years. In a dozen worldwide centres, Rei Kawakubo of Comme des Garçons, and her partner Adrian Joffe (who is an architect) are opening then closing their aptly named Guerrilla Stores in exactly one year time-slots.

Comme des Garçons is using local architects for its 'guerrilla' tactics, people who know their cities better than do international firms who just fly in and fly out, although even the big names in boutiques attempt to adjust their design to local conditions. Architect William Sofield for Gucci comments: "Within global rollout, each store is city-specific." For the Fifth Avenue Gucci boutique in New York, he says by way of example, "there is a sense of exaggeration."[34]

If you are a fashion designer with a hundred or so shops, each is of course special, but to maintain exclusivity and avoid over-branding some must be exceptional. Jil Sander seeks out homes for her flagship boutiques in historic structures, landmark buildings, palazzi. Prada creates unpredictability and variability, inviting a selection of star architects to design spectacular buildings.

Location is everything, and boutiques create the most prestigious streets in the fashion capitals – Bond Street, London; Montenapoleone, Milan; Madison Avenue, New York; avenue Montaigne, Paris; Omotesando, Tokyo. However, many fashion designers enjoy an attention-grabbing alternative, setting up shop in fringe districts, luring clients into 'forbidden' neighbourhoods for that added touch of *frisson*. Carlos Miele, Stella McCartney and Alexander McQueen, for example, have their new boutiques in the meatpacking district of New York, in the same block on West 14th Street. "I like to do things different from other people," remarks McQueen. "There's no traffic in the meatpacking area – in fashion, we call people 'traffic', all the people walking past your shop, like on Madison Avenue. But I think it adds atmosphere to my work if it's in a strange area. Even at night, when you've got the prostitutes, it's inspiring to me."[35]

As culture becomes infinitely disseminated, as boundaries blur between retail and fashion and art and design, the new boutique becomes more than a boutique. Architects are not just architects of boutiques; they are interdisciplinary, their approach carrying through from one building type to another. Herzog & de Meuron designed not only Tokyo Prada but London's Tate Modern art gallery and the 2008 Olympic stadium in Beijing.[36] Jean-Michel Wilmotte, architect of the Paris John Galliano boutique, is respected as an architect of many fine art galleries. So is Richard Gluckman, who creates all of Helmut Lang's boutiques. In the boutiques that these architects design, as in most new boutiques, garments are displayed like museum objects – which these items might well become, as prestigious museums collect and exhibit fashion pieces and mount fashion designer retrospectives.[37] Many of the new boutiques have fitted artworks, such as the running LED installations by Jenny Holzer in the Helmut Lang boutiques,

Issey Miyake Fete, Tokyo: An installation by artist Kenji Yanobe, part of the boutique's interior design from 2002 to 2004, featured a reptilian mannequin and Queen Mamma fitting room.

the three-storey mural by Jeff Koons in the Hugo Boss on Fifth Avenue, the Carsten Höller dressing room projections in Dior Tokyo Omotesando. And there are the weekly boutique rounds of rotating exhibitions, music recitals and performance works.

The new boutique is the new, beautiful, private–public space. Outside Herzog & de Meuron's Tokyo Prada you can meet your friends in the little public garden, such a rarity in that city. Or you can unwind, literally, on the blood-red spinning stools in the shopping decompression chamber of Comme des Garçons in Paris. At the Kenzo flagship in Paris, have a tickle and a massage in the *bulles*, the 'bubbles' of LaBulleKenzo, before nipping upstairs to the Philippe Starck restaurant, or downstairs for sushi and e-mails in front of the banks of computer screens. In Milan, at Dolce & Gabanna Men's, buy a new tie, get a haircut and a close shave at the barber's, hit the grooming salon, then meet that someone special for a cocktail at the Martini and Rossi bar, designed by Ferruccio Laviani like a luxurious opium den.

Design for the 2008 Olympic stadium, Beijing. The architects Herzog & de Meuron (working with Arup and CAG as engineer and sports architecture) assert that their design for the Prada Epicenter in Tokyo was "a laboratory" of ideas for the stadium.

NOTES

1 Conversation with the author, 1 July 2004.

2 See Karen Franck, 'Yes, we wear buildings', in *Architectural Design*, vol. 70, December 2000, pp. 94–97.

3 Martin M. Pegler, *Visual Merchandising and Display*, New York (Fairchild Books & Visuals) 4th edition, 1998, p. 3.

4 Caroline Rennolds Milbank, *Couture: The Great Designers*, New York (Stewart, Tabori & Chang) 1985, p. 69.

5 The proliferation of architect-designed boutiques in France c.1890–1910 prompted the lavishly illustrated publication *Devantures de boutiques et installations de magasins: façades et détails, intérieurs, détails de construction, coupes, plans, assemblages*, Paris (Ducher) n.d. (c.1911), 2nd edition n.d. (c.1922).

6 Mary McLeod, 'Undressing Architecture: Fashion, Gender and Modernity', in Deborah Fausch, Paulette Singley, Rodolphe El-Khoury and Zvi Efrat (eds.), *Architecture: In Fashion*, Princeton, NJ (Princeton Architectural Press) 1994, p. 76. Mark Wigley in his *White Walls, Designer Dresses: The Fashioning of Modern Architecture*, Cambridge, Mass (MIT Press) 1995, contends that the Modernists, although textually rejecting fashion, in practice followed contemporary reforms in clothing design, adopting them as part of their architectural aesthetic. No matter how thin the white coat of paint, "it is itself a very particular form of clothing" (p. xviii).

7 L.P. Sézille, *Devantures de boutiques*, Paris (Editions Albert Lévy) 1927.

8 Roger Poulain, *Boutiques 1931*, Paris (Vincent Freal) 1931. Poulain also wrote and collected *Boutiques 1929*, Paris (Vincent Freal) 1929.

9 René Herbst, *Boutiques et magasins*, Paris (Moreau) n.d. (c.1928) n.p. (Introduction). Also in his series was *Nouvelles devantures et agencements de magasins parisiens*, n.d. (c.1926); *Nouvelles devantures et agencements de magasins*, Paris (Moreau), n.d. (c.1927); in English, *Modern French Shop-fronts and Their Interiors*, London (John Tiranti) 1927. From the same years, but taking a more antiquarian approach, using traditional and new examples, but with little of the Modernism promulgated by the French, was Frederick Chatterton, *Shop Fronts: A Selection of English, American and Continental Examples*, London (Architectural Press) 1927. And with a distinctly anti-Modern approach – "this Utopia of architectural nihilism which M. Le Corbusier has conceived" (p. 58) – was A. Trystan Edwards, *The Architecture of Shops*, London (Chapman & Hall) 1933, although he did illustrate what we now consider to be Modern examples such as Wells Coates's Cresta shop interior, Brighton, England (plate L).

10 'Moth treatment' was the term the architect Morris Lapidus gave to the placement of bright lights to make shoppers stop in front of merchandise or draw them in to the back of a boutique. Lapidus, a prolific designer of boutiques in mid-twentieth-century America, also recalled in the usual irreverent approach he took in his autobiography, that during the 1930s he "tried everything. Pilasters were topped by carved female figures or jazzed up modern whatnots. The cornices were embellished with carved moldings in the latest hopped-up modern. The floor plans for the merchandise case were tortured and twisted. The merchants were ready for every kooky idea as long as it could be called modern." Morris Lapidus, *Too Much Is Never Enough*, New York (Rizzoli) 1996, pp. 88, 100.

11 Robert Aloi, *Esempi: di architettura moderna de tutto il mondo*, Milan (Ulrico Hoepli) 1950, with text in Italian, French and German. See also Lesley Jackson, *The New Look: Design in the Fifties*, London (Thames and Hudson) 1991 for a study of the links between the female figure, exaggerated women's fashion and object design in the 1950s.

12 Jose A. Fernandez, *The Speciality Shop: A Guide*, New York (Architectural Book Publishing) 1950.

13 Marnie Fogg, *Boutique: A '60s Cultural Phenomenon*, London (Mitchell Beazley) 2003; Lesley Jackson, *The Sixties: Decade of Design Revolution*, London (Phaidon) 1998, esp. 'The consumer revolution', pp. 34–53; Kate McIntyre, 'The most "In" shops for gear', in *Twentieth Century Architecture 6: The sixties – life: style: architecture*, London (The Twentieth Century Society) 2002, pp. 36–46.

14 *Domus*, December 1970, no. 493, pp. 24–25. Shiro Kuramata created a series of boutiques for the fashion designer Issey Miyake in the 1980s. See Arata Isozaki, Ettore Sottsass *et. al.*, *Shiro Kuramata, 1934–91*, Tokyo (Foundation Arc-en-ciel) 1996.

15 Alice Rawsthorn, *Yves Saint Laurent*, London (Harper Collins) 1996, pp. 86–89.

16 Ettore Sottsass *et al.*, *Sottsass Associati*, New York (Rizzoli) 1988.

17 The finest review of 1980s boutiques is by Brigitte Fitoussi, published simultaneously in French and English: *Boutiques*, Paris (Moniteur) 1989, and *Showrooms*, Princeton, NJ (Princeton University Press) 1989.

18 Jose Manser, *The Joseph Shops: London 1983–1989: Eva Jiricna*, London (Architecture Design and Technology Press) 1991.

19 Lisa Freedman, 'Hamnett in SW3; Architects: Norman Foster', in *Blueprint*, November 1986, pp. 34–37.

20 The year following the opening of his New York Calvin Klein boutique on Madison Avenue, John Pawson published his quiet architectural agenda: *Minimum*, London (Phaidon) 1996.

21 Conversation with the author, 19 July 2004.

22 Teri Agins, *The End of Fashion: The Mass Marketing of the Clothing Business*, New York (William Morrow) 1999.

23 Chuihua Judy Chung, Jeffrey Inaba, Rem Koolhaas, Sze Tsung Leong (eds.), *Harvard Design School guide to shopping*, Cologne (Taschen) 2001.

24 Rem Koolhass & OMA, *Projects for Prada. Part 1*, Milan (Fondazione Prada Edizioni) 2001.

25 Herzog & de Meuron, *Prada Aoyama Tokyo*, Milan (Progetto Prada Arte) 2004.

26 Ron Kaal, 'The great equalizer', in *Frame*, no. 38, May–June 2004, pp. 56–57. "Retail architecture feeds on the blood of everything available – art and technology, ideas and culture – not for the purpose of producing something permanent, but of creating a permanent state of volatility. On completion, it is already doomed to die."

27 See Bradley Quinn, *The Fashion of Architecture*, London (Berg) 2003, an extremely perceptive investigation into the contemporary relationship between fashion and architecture.

28 Correspondence with the author, May 2004. Ferré received his degree in Architecture from the Politecnico di Milano in 1969. Similar sentiments were voiced by the fashion designer Pierre Balmain (1914–82) who took architecture at the Ecole des Beaux-Arts in Paris during the early 1930s, but left his studies to work for the couturier Edward Molyneux: "Un vêtement se construit comme un edifice." (A piece of clothing is created in the same way as a building.) "La couture, c'est l'architecture du movement." (Fashion is architecture in motion.) Quoted in an interview with Pierre Balmain by Carine Lenfant in *Architecture (Revue de L'Ordre des Architectes)*, April 1981, no. 24, pp. 36–37.

29 Correspondence with the author, May 2004.

30 Charlotte Vaudrey, 'On the road to the shrine', in *Frame*, January/February 2003, no. 30, pp. 52–63. Eric Carlson, one of the two principal architects for Louis Vuitton, persuaded the LV board to accept the industrial materials such as the mesh by referring to them as 'fabrics'.

31 Conversation with the author, 12 July 2004.

32 Conversation with the author, 3 June 2004.

33 No. 10, door on the right.

34 Quoted in Julia Lewis, 'Sexissimo!', in *Interior Design*, January 2001, no. 4.

35 Quoted in Ariel Levy, 'Alexander the Great', in www.newyorkmetro.com/shopping/articles/02/fallfashion/alexandermcqueen, visited 31 July 2004. Not everyone was pleased about the new proliferation of fashion designers in the meatpacking district. In the television programme *Sex in the City* (which between 1998 and 2004 popularized fashion, fashion designers and the new boutique more than any other programme of the period) the character of Samantha, who had moved to the meatpacking district to escape the Upper East Side, complains: "Just look at this street! Stella McCartney, Alexander McQueen … the only designer name that belongs in the meatpacking district is Oscar Mayer," referring to the famous hot dog. Her girlfriend Carrie replies, "I never liked his clothes. Too fatty." (Sixth series, episode 'To market, to market'.)

36 Jacques Herzog, 'Herzog & de Meuron: Prada and new projects', Architecture Foundation lecture delivered at the Union Chapel, Islington, London, 10 December 2003.

37 In 2000, the exhibition *Giorgio Armani: a retrospective* launched at the Solomon R Guggenheim Museum in New York, with the interior spiralling ramp of the Frank Lloyd Wright building swathed in white gauze by artist Robert Wilson – the museum as a clothed body. The exhibition travelled in 2003 to the Royal Academy of Arts, London, the first major exhibition on fashion in the venerable Academy's 235-year history.

LONDON

Jil Sander
Michael Gabellini

Maison Martin Margiela
Maison Martin Margiela

Mandarina Duck
Marcel Wanders/Harper & McKay

Marni
Sybarite

Matthew Williamson
Matthew Williamson/Claire Ceprynski

Oki-ni
6a Architects

Jil Sander

Burlington Gardens
London

Michael Gabellini

In the heart of London's Mayfair is an aristocratic powerhouse of fashion and architecture. Rising on the corner of Burlington Gardens and Savile Row, just a few steps from the Burlington Arcade, is Queensberry House, a large eighteenth-century townhouse that architect Michael Gabellini has exquisitely restored and adapted as the Jil Sander boutique.

The fashion designer Jil Sander has a penchant for collecting beautiful historic buildings. And Gabellini has the touch to give them a new life, with a modern twist. Sander's headquarters in Hamburg, Germany, is a nineteenth-century lakeside villa. Her New York boutique is in a landmark building on the Upper East Side; in Paris on avenue Montaigne she

has a great Beaux-Arts pile; in Munich, Berlin, Milan – Gabellini floats his boutique interiors within the architectural fabric, complementing and enhancing but never interfering with the historic structure.

Gabellini began working with Jil Sander in 1993, and since then Gabellini Associates have notched up nearly one hundred shops for her company. The stylistic alliance fits as neatly as one of the designer's much admired suits. Jil Sander is the byword in tailoring for the working woman – those who can afford her: dresses and trouser suits that are reserved, understated, luxurious in fabric. She makes no big fashion statements, no gesture to fantasy. Just simplicity and quality ... like a Gabellini interior.

Left The grand eighteenth-century staircase leads to the VIP reception rooms on the first floor. **Above** The nineteenth-century banking hall was transformed by Michael Gabellini into the principal retail space.

Top right The main façade of Queensberry House, Burlington Gardens, today the flagship Jil Sander London boutique. **Right** Low, curving dividing panels and hanging racks barely touch the historic fabric of the building.

Lying behind a single Portland stone façade, Jil Sander's London boutique is in fact in two sections. The principal room is an enormous double-height space, a former banking hall for the Bank of England, added on to the old house in the 1870s by P.C. Hardwick, the architect of Paddington Station. Here the main collection is displayed, discreetly and beautifully.

The space is spacious and bright, with light pouring in through the large windows on two sides and from the four great round skylights. For those dull London days and winter evenings, there are fine lines of halogens inserted into the ceiling beams. The walls are painted an eggshell white, the floor is of Italian limestone.

Gabellini's display of Jil Sander's range is like an art installation set in a *galleria*. Low serpentine walls weave between the gold-burnished Ionic columns. These walls give sense to the differing parts of the collection, act as backdrops for the mannequins and clasp wafer-thin shelves made of nickel-silver housing a neat strip of under-lighting. Display racks hang acrobatically from the ceiling beams, lean against the walls, and rise from the floor on thin metal stems.

The second section of the boutique is in the grand rooms of the original house, designed between 1721 and 1723 by Giacomo Leoni and with later alterations and additions by John Vardy the Younger and Joseph Bonomi in the 1780s.

These rooms, which serve as an extension of the collection on the ground floor and VIP lounges on the first, are among the finest London interiors for their periods, with ceilings delicately plastered in ornamental patterns. Gabellini again has kept a tight control on his intervention, for example, positioning his mirrored changing screens in the centre of the room.

The old house pivots around a glorious staircase, with a double dome decorated by Joseph Rose, Robert Adam's favourite plasterer. Gabellini had ten coats of paint cleaned off the banister and wrought-iron balustrades. And, down its centre, he has hung a 5.5 m (18 ft) tubular chandelier of his own design – a ray of light.

Left A private reception room on the first floor of the Jil Sander London boutique, with its beautifully restored, intricately patterned eighteenth-century stucco ceiling. **Above** Michael Gabellini's tubular chandelier drops from the centre of the staircase dome. **Right** Pivoting mirror walls in a private fitting room.

Maison Martin Margiela

Bruton Place
London

Maison Martin Margiela

This is Maison Martin Margiela – the boutique, the designer ... where white is beautiful ... and anonymous ... and synonymous.

Confused? Actually, it is all very simple. The Belgian-born fashion designer Martin Margiela attempts to keep himself as anonymous as his shops. Even to his adoring public, he has no face. Unlike his fellow designers who are seen daily in the press hanging off the arms of Hollywood stars and beautiful supermodels, Margiela is not and does not. He rarely appears at his own fashion shows – when, that is, he stages them. For one season, by way of an example, the press and fashion cognoscenti found themselves in rather seedy Paris betting bars, viewing grainy recordings of the Maison Martin Margiela new collection worn by fairly ordinary young men and women going about their fairly ordinary young lives. Like travelling on the Metro ... which Margiela does, anonymously.

He even refers to himself as Maison Martin Margiela, implying that he is but one of the staff. And everyone in his boutiques wears white lab coats: a uniform not of uniformity but rather of co-operative solidarity mixed with a dash of aesthetic equality to make them blend into their surroundings.

The majority of Martin Margiela's collections are monochrome, simple and beautifully constructed. Part of his line is, in a sense, recycled: old clothes are taken apart and then reconstructed – *vêtements transformés (artisanal)*, as he calls them, 'garments remodelled by hand'. The name of the fashion house does not even appear on the inner clothing label. Just rows of numbers, with specific ones circled to indicate the line.

As architectural metaphors for the house style, his boutiques keep a low profile. A roughly painted, handwritten sign for Maison Martin Margiela is stuck to a wall at the entrance to the little mews street in London's Mayfair. It's just off New Bond Street, right round the corner from Stella McCartney and many of the big fashion

Opposite, top The frosted skylight and windows of the former artists' studio illuminate the collection. Opposite, bottom White, bright, simple and anonymous. Below, clockwise from top left Recycled nineteenth-century doors beneath the wooden beams of the original stable building; clients are invited to leave their own graffiti contributions; white paint and distressed surfaces. Right The distinctive garment labelling of Maison Martin Margiela.

houses. The sign looks temporary, but it's not. The boutique is just down along the way, unmarked, its signboard whitewashed over. At least this is some sort of pointer: to find the two Paris shops you have to wind down the back alley behind the Palais Royal and then along an unmarked passageway; in Tokyo the boutique is up on the third floor of an anonymous-looking apartment building.

The London boutique is in an old stable block, converted over a century ago into artists' studios, and then into a fine-art gallery. It is filled with natural light. So, with everything painted white, from furniture to floorboards, and the collections being mainly white, this is a bright, cheerful place. The walls are left rough, the timber-trussed beams exposed. The fixtures and fittings are mainly second-hand: mismatching chairs, travelling trunks. The changing room doors, with pretty mouldings, are from old Parisian apartments. The collections are displayed on simple racks and coarsely made wooden display stands, in large plastic tube ends, or just pinned to the wall. The service point is two French supermarket check-out stands.

The only mannequins in the boutique are the two bound together by a simple single fitted white cotton garment. They stand united as the symbol of Maison Martin Margiela's focus on the clothes, anonymous as the wrapped faces of the models in his fashion shows. This boutique, with its graffiti room for visitors to scribble on the walls what they will, and its cheap old furniture and its white paint camouflage is, as one of its lab-coated staff so aptly pointed out, "Maison Martin Margiela's way to erase the shop."

Mandarina Duck

Conduit Street
London

Marcel Wanders / Harper & McKay

Temple of sculpture or high-class porn shop? An amusing mix of both impressions greets you on your first visit to the Mandarina Duck boutique in London. That the designer Marcel Wanders is Dutch, from Amsterdam, should therefore come as no surprise, for his is a city famous for nurturing the fine arts alongside the pleasures of the body. And, aren't art and the body what fashion is basically about?

The boutique is populated by a small army of clones: dozens of mannequins, both male and female, muscular and defined, bald and in the Mandarina Duck corporate colour of marigold yellow. In the centre, rising through two storeys, is their leader, 6.5 m (21 ft) tall, a figure reminiscent of Michelangelo's *David*. From the ground floor, we see him from the waist down, in all his anatomical glory. From the first floor, he gazes at us impassively. His minions – some clothed, others *au naturel* – stand guard, determined but gently breathing with life.

Breathing? The effect is pure Marcel Wanders, the clever humorist. "I like to make things light and with a sense of humour," says the designer, "but never a joke." And so the silver chests of the mannequins are designed to rise and fall, to 'breathe'.

The big fella, Wanders is keen to point out, is his interpretation of Gulliver from the classic eighteenth-century tale *Gulliver's Travels* by Jonathan Swift. Near the end of his book, the author admonishes his readers with the caution: "My principal Design was to Inform, and not to amuse thee." In Mandarina Duck, however, our Gulliver both informs and amuses. And he is a traveller; in fact, we could say that he is the travelling salesman for this Italian company, which first made its name as a purveyor of luggage and handbags. The boutique even sells a unique handbag designed by Wanders, made with temperature-sensitive materials that have been heated to inflate, like a pufferfish does when it is threatened.

Below Clothed and unclothed marigold-yellow mannequins gaze impassively out of the picture window.
Opposite The tubular steel staircase, which has echoes of those found in cruise liners, is backed by a wall of silvery panels that undulate and 'breathe'.

Wanders was assisted in his design by the London architects Harper & McKay, who helped to create a shop interior of pleasant elegance. Cases are made of smoked-glass boxes with clear cases on top, often jauntily overhanging the edges. Mirrors are freestanding, oversized and framed in wide yellow borders. The tubular metal staircase takes a nice curve, past wall panels of a specially made silvery paper by DuPont which, again, are made to undulate, to 'breathe'.

The London Mandarina Duck is what the company calls 'an embassy', one of its most select stores. Droog Design and NL architects did the very stylish yet spare Paris boutique. And in Rome, Angelo Micheli created an embassy interior lit by zigzagging neon tubes and cloth-covered chandeliers. Different stores with different designers means different styles, a way of keeping clients interested. Mandarina Duck is not aiming for branding consistency through its boutique image. Rather, if you will excuse the pun, it tries to breathe new life into each project.

Below The giant figure of Gulliver, his legs spotted with sound speakers, rises through an opening to the first floor. **Opposite, top** Marcel Wanders's 'Light Shade Shade' chandeliers. **Opposite, bottom** The mannequins' chests hide a mechanism that imitates the action of breathing.

Marni

Sloane Street
London

Sybarite

The London Marni is a boutique of extraordinary energy, cutting-edge technology and design innovation. The space burns with such radiance that it makes you want to pluck the sunglasses out of those specially designed wall pockets and pop them on as protection.

A long, sinuous silver line explodes near the entrance, whips up alongside the staircase, splits and throws itself in two directions … and then unfurls. But what is this continuous piece of sculpture that grows like high-tech clematis? It is the clothing rail. Yes, the humble rail, the basic instrument of garment display, the very essence of every rag shop from Calcutta to Anchorage. In Marni, however, the rail has morphed into a

retail art form. As the London boutique is the largest in Marni's worldwide network, Sybarite's designers have been able to take the rail to its most extenuated development.

Torquil McIntosh, who along with Simon Mitchell is principal partner of Sybarite, formerly worked in the architectural offices of Future Systems. Their design is in the next generation of this high-tech firm, which did many of the previous Marni boutiques. The progression seems seamless.

Made of highly polished stainless steel, the rail frame begins on the ground floor, anchored in an undulating flat form reminiscent of an arched rattlesnake about to strike. These level surfaces are

Opposite The undulating structure of the polished stainless steel clothing rail forms a continuous fluid line in, up, around and throughout both levels of the boutique.
Right, top Evenly spaced hooks on the clothing rail ensure that each item of the collection is consistently displayed.
Right, bottom The flat pedestals, which act as weighted counterbalances for the rack structure, can also be used as display tables.

for displaying accessories. Out of this spring three lines of rails: two cascade in a loop out into the shop, ending in yet another flat display surface hovering above the floor; the other whiplashes up to the first floor, where the tubing divides. One section stretches into the room at the front, where it bursts forth into a formation of rails and shelving similar to that below. The other section veers off to the rear, dipping down towards the floor to take the shoe display, and then up again for clothes.

"By making the rail sculptural," says McIntosh, "we respect the language of the boutique, but turn it on its head." It is all part of the successful attempt to create a space 'with no structure'. Of course, the structure is there, but either it seems lighter than air – like the rack that is designed so as to make it appear to float – or it is inverted, like the staircase, the other major feature of this boutique.

In boutiques, staircases normally make a great statement; they have to, because a prime part of their job is to lure and draw the customer up, or down, and thus further into the shop. They stand out, their structure placed proud, steps on parade. Here in the London Marni, however, the staircase is sunk, dropped into a red elliptical slot, swallowed by the curve of the white body of the floor which slips into becoming the rear wall, part of the anti-structural game. Yet the staircase is not only beautiful, but alluring, with its pin-blasted matt steel treads and looping handrail.

The interior of the boutique has large cuts: red into white in the floors, white into red in the ceilings. The carpeting is poppy, inset in the sunken spaces around the seating areas with their crescent seats, "like blades hovering," comments McIntosh. The lighting is concealed in the overhead clouds. There are even sunken holes within the entrance doors of the boutique. Luckily there is a friendly, handsome boutique bouncer with a "Watch your step" to assist you in.

Above and opposite London Marni's spectacular stainless steel staircase and clothing rail is the craftwork of the Italian metalwork firm of Marzorati Ronchetti, from the design of the architects, Sybarite. The stair treads are pitted by pin-blasting.

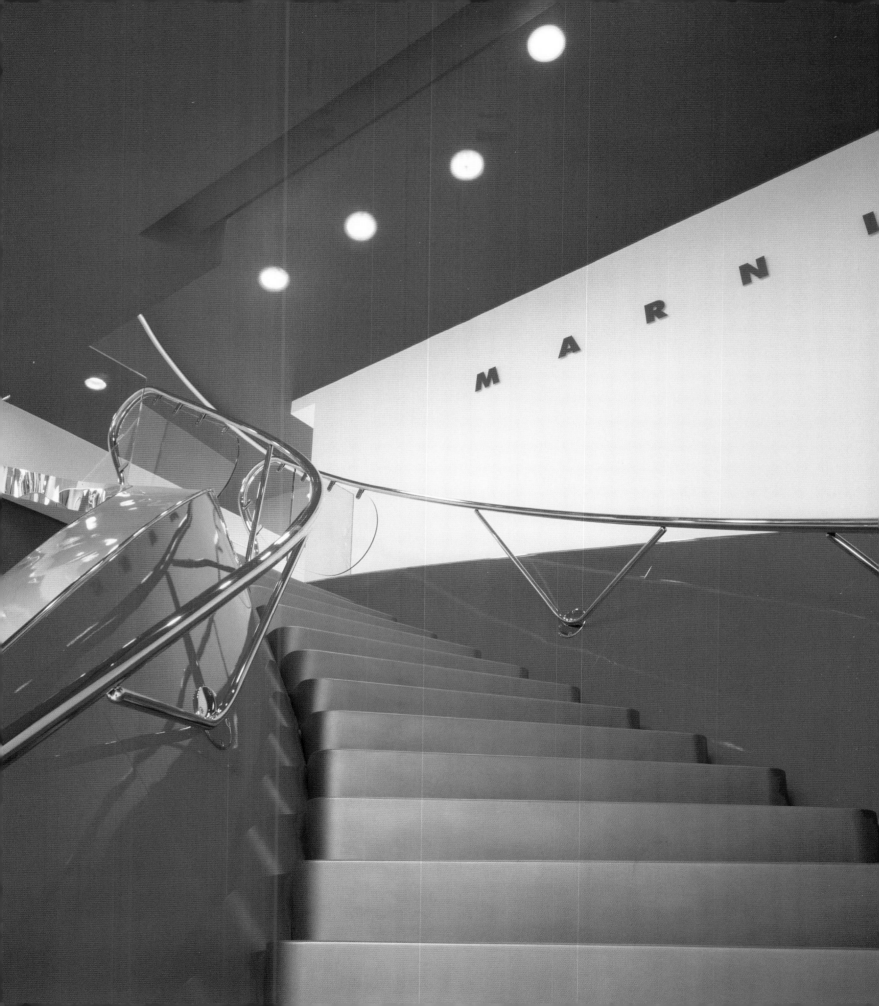

Matthew Williamson

Bruton Street
London

Matthew Williamson / Claire Ceprynski

The strip of hot lipstick-pink signage over Matthew Williamson's boutique in the heart of London's Mayfair tips you off that there is something sizzling within. All that heat and intensity … well, that seems just so un-British. But then, as a designer, the Englishman Matthew Williamson is known for his brightly coloured and exotic fashions, what he calls 'celebratory clothes', outfits found at the end of a rainbow. And in grey old London, there are very few days with rainbows.

This is Matthew Williamson's first shop, and although it is set in a conservative brick eighteenth-century townhouse, he and his boutique co-designer, installation artist Claire Ceprynski, have adapted it to reflect the designer's spicy look. The fine historic cornice, panelling and skirting decoration have been painted off-white, in tune with the creamy stone floor of Turkish travertine. Against this neutrality flashes the colour of the clothing and the interior furnishings. The rails, in shocking orange and acid lemon, are set in the floor. Lines of boxed scented candles descend in candy columns of colour. The semicircular service desk is in the highest of high gloss, and in that signature hot pink.

At the front of the shop hang three different but similar early twentieth-century chandeliers of deeply tinted Murano glass. From each of them is suspended a mannequin. "This is my reinterpretation of the caryatids," says Ceprynski,

Above The boutique's vibrant colours brighten up the pavement of venerable old Mayfair. **Right** The dressing-room mirror reflects the 'garden tank' filled with an artificial tropical garden. **Opposite, top** The colourful rails and service desk are as hot and spicy as the designer's clothing. **Opposite, bottom** Mannequins are suspended from vintage Italian glass chandeliers.

thinking of the Classical Greek female figures of the Erechtheion in Athens. The figures hover over circular perspex tables, lit from within, that act as stands for accessories.

A great influence on Matthew Williamson's style is his travels to the Far East, whose sights, sounds and smells waft into his designs. The rear section of the boutique is like something brought back from one of these excursions. The walls are wrapped in sensational silk chinoiserie wallpaper, designed by De Gournay. On a background of deep green, hand-painted birds of paradise frolic between large patterned flowers. Williamson has added small pieces of costume jewellery, held in the birds' beaks, or little three-dimensional butterflies alongside painted versions, the butterfly being a favourite motif appearing on his clothes.

But the *pièce de résistance* is the 'garden tank', a large glass-enclosed box brimming with plants, a palm tree and orchids. You can almost feel the heat, the lushness, the scent. It's a minor miracle, because all the foliage is *faux*. The natural light from the skylight contributes to the illusion.

Behind is a second box, almost the size of the tank, housing the dressing rooms, and also naturally lit from above. The garden thus allows the dressing rooms to be obscured, but not hidden. The outer walls of this box are mirrored, an effect which is carried through to the bevelled mirrors and mirror-glass console table just outside the rooms. But within the dressing rooms the theme returns to colour, with carpeting in a rich plum colour and Day-Glo yellow chairs upholstered in purple silk and chiffon flowers and leaves.

The Matthew Williamson boutique is not architect-led in its design, although architects were called in to make the detailed drawings. Rather, it is an example of a fashion designer and an in-sync friend and colleague working through the fashion design vision into a boutique vocabulary.

Oki-ni

Savile Row
London

6a Architects

London's Savile Row is the famous heart of British tailoring. It may be historic, but it has kept pace with the times. Many of the tip top tailors here are young and original – Timothy Everest, Ozwald Boateng, Richard James – with dapper shops to match. At the lower end of the street – where eighteenth-century houses turn into twentieth-century office blocks – is an interloper. Oki-ni is not a tailor, but it is certainly as exclusive as any of those pinstripe suit parlours.

Oki-ni (the Japanese for a politeness somewhere between 'please' and 'thank you') is a cyberspace boutique, part of the bubble-bursting world of net retail. Most business for Oki-ni is carried out online, with loyal customers logging on to the company's website and then paging through a range of small edition clothes by top-name brands and designers such as Evisu, Gavin Turk, 25 Porter, Paul Smith, Griffin, even Timothy Everest from up the road. All the designs, reads the website, "are produced in strictly limited numbers to maintain rarity and uniqueness", and made by Oki-ni.

Scotsman Paddy Meehan, the e-tailor retailer behind Oki-ni, considers his boutique to be a gallery for his dot.com commerce, a place where his clients can drop in for a dose of reality browsing.

"[Paddy Meehan] wants the store to be more permanent than the way the product is usually sold," explains Tom Emerson, one of the

Opposite The architects describe their Oki-ni boutique as a 'tray insert' in a concrete shell, with the Russian oak floor and low-rise walls standing proud of the existing building fabric. **Left** View of the shop from Savile Row, with the almost imperceptible incline of the boutique floor, like a stage, echoing the slope of the street. **Below** The collection hangs off the wooden perimeter wall like washing slung over a fence.

trio of architects – alongside Stephanie Macdonald and Lee Marsden – who make up 6a Architects, designers of the Oki-ni boutique. Nevertheless, the architects received a brief from Meehan stating that the space was to be like an installation, 'placed', transient. The result, as Emerson says of the design, is a boutique which is 'an object in space'.

And you can see this. The interior of the shop floats within its walls, as the architects maintain, "like a tray insert". The large space has been cleared completely, right back to the concrete shell, and then the irregularly shaped wooden tray slotted in: the sides a 2.1 m (7 ft) perimeter fence, the flooring of the same Russian oak boarding. The spaces between the permanent concrete walls and the wooden enclosure are used for changing rooms and storage. "The effect", smiles Emerson, "is as if the tray has never adjusted entirely to its host building."

The view from the street is a good one. The three display windows of the 1950s building are so expansive that the entire uncluttered interior can be observed in one go. Moreover, the floor has been given a gentle incline – an echo of the outside pavement on Savile Row – causing the contents to become a large stage.

To maintain the impression of a gallery of clothes, the architects speak of the fittings and furnishings as 'installations'. There are no racks. Garments are slung over the wooden fence walls, or on hangers simply hooked to the fence top. There are no display tables, just piles of felt matting with merchandise arranged on their soft and giving surfaces; little bulb lamps hang overhead. And there is no point of sale. Staff shift their laptops around, perching them on little metal shelves attached to the walls, sitting on the matting.

This casual ambience certainly seems a long way away from the digital high-tech world that actually underlies this boutique.

MILAN

Armani Centre

Michael Gabellini

Dolce & Gabbana

David Chipperfield/Ferruccio Laviani

Gianfranco Ferré

Gianfranco Ferré/Michael Gabellini

Giorgio Armani

Claudio Silvestrin

Miss Sixty

Studio 63 Architecture and Design

Moschino

Sean Dix

Paul Smith

Sophie Hicks

Piombo

Ferruccio Laviani

Armani Centre

via Manzoni
Milan

Michael Gabellini

"The space is rhythmic, compositional and proportional. Like an Armani jacket," comments the architect Michael Gabellini about his design of the Armani Centre, Milan. "It also has authority, masculinity … for it is within one of the finest 1930s Modernist buildings in Italy."

At the end of the most fashionable of all Milan streets, via Montenapoleone, is indeed the solid and masculine former Assicurazioni Generali building, designed by Enrico A. Griffini in 1937, with its three lightly clad sculptural figures of the patron saints of Milan, Venice and Trieste gazing placidly at passing shoppers. The interior has been transformed by Gabellini into a Giorgio Armani galaxy. This is the boutique as department store, on three levels, covering some 8000 sq. m (86,000 sq ft), a place where the visitor can find the major Armani lines in clothing, accessories and perfumes. There is also a home furnishing section, a flower shop, a confectionery counter, a bookstore, restaurants and a bar. On the lower level is a Sony electronics gallery, designed by Studio C+. It's all an Armani lifestyle experience, as the PR people say.

The image of Armani is one of a mature, timeless style. "Change has to be subtle," the designer once remarked. "When a woman alters her look too much from season to season, she becomes a fashion victim." Armani opened his first boutique in Milan in 1975. By the early 1980s he had conquered America and was a household fashion name. He creates high fashion for Hollywood stars and year after year his dresses and tuxedos appear on the red carpet at the Academy Awards; and for the rest of us mere earthlings he epitomizes the sophisticated casual.

The length of the building is bisected by what the designer and architect refer to as an internal street, a modern echo of Milan's famous glass-roofed Galleria Vittorio Emanuele. Paving is in granite and beige quartz; the great pillars are faced with Turkish Supai stone. The overall impression is cool and classical, as you might

Top left The long row of display windows at the Armani Centre. **Left** Bands of fabric stretch above a circular atrium, diffusing the light as it flows in. **Bottom left** The suspended bridge walkway cuts dramatically across a second, square atrium. **Opposite, top and bottom** Michael Gabellini has transformed what was an insurance-company building into a small department store of free-flowing spaces to display the major Armani lines.

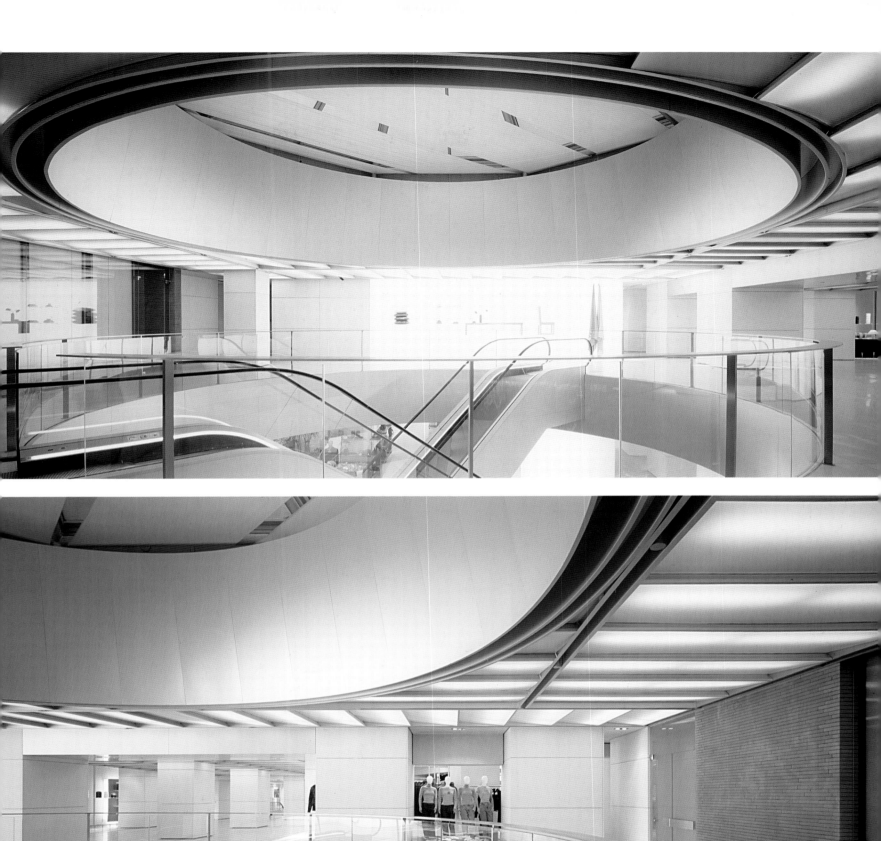

From fashion to flowers, cafés to chocolates, the Armani Centre is an emporium of luxury. Large LED screens are placed throughout the store, thin metal shelving is suspended from the ceiling, ceiling panels and merchandise counters glow with light from within; in the café, the suspended balcony makes a dramatic impact.

imagine the rich white marble interiors of ancient Rome to have been. However, there are no togas here … as you cross the threshold, you are hit, and mesmerized, by an enormous LED wall screen with beautiful men and women strutting the Armani catwalk.

At either end of the building are the escalator atriums, in which natural light is diffused through wide textile panels: one atrium is circular, while the other is rectangular and has a courtyard effect with the added touch of a suspended bridge walkway across it, not a recommended short cut for the acrophobic.

The spaces between the different collections are allowed to flow freely. This is not a line of mall shops. Differentiation is subtle, with each collection shown in an apt and distinct design capsule. The Emporio section radiates light. Translucent boxed lights are suspended from the ceiling and inset into merchandizing counters and seating. Windows are screened with plexiglas curtains. Shelving is extremely elegant, undulating stainless steel and wood laminated surfaces that seem to hang in the balance. More rugged is the Armani Jeans section, with exposed fluorescent ceiling lights and tents as changing rooms. The bookshop has wooden shelves, in some sections their finishes left natural to give a traditional library feel, in others painted white and set against an illuminated wall for a sense of novelty.

The Nobu restaurant, one of a series under the illustrious Japanese-meets-South American cuisine of chef Nobuyuki Matsuhisa, extends the building's theme of the illuminated screen, with the appropriate touch of bamboo. The sushi bar, too, has a backlit surface, in mottled onyx.

Dolce & Gabbana

Corso Venezia
Milan

David Chipperfield / Ferruccio Laviani

It feels like any moment now the tall, handsome figure of Burt Lancaster is going to come strolling through the grand rooms of this fashionable Milanese men's boutique. Doesn't this seem like one of those dazzling locations in Visconti's film *The Leopard*, in which Lancaster's nineteenth-century Sicilian prince strides formidably through the Baroque splendour of his several palazzi?

The Baroque period and the Sicilian connection – both are strong stylistic references in the work of the fashion duo Domenico Dolce and Stefano Gabbana. Dolce is from just outside Palermo in Sicily, where he studied fashion design and worked in his family's small clothing business. And although Gabbana is a Milanese, he too has

become seduced by the Sicilian spell. And you can't love Sicily without loving the ornate lavishness of its Baroque art and architecture. Sometimes in their collections, Dolce & Gabbana allude to Sicilian costume and tradition. And in their boutiques, this fun-loving couple enjoy placing flamboyant Baroque pieces of furniture into modern settings: the great pair of gold and red thrones found in most of their boutiques is just such a bit of showmanship.

When Dolce & Gabbana acquired the magnificent late eighteenth-century Palazzo Labus in Milan's most fashionable district, they worked with two architects for its transformation into their flagship men's boutique. One was David

Above A nineteenth-century painting of a male nude hangs in the shoe department on the mezzanine level, reinforcing the masculinity of the collection. **Opposite** Within the grand fresco-ceiling rooms of the Palazzo Labus, restored by David Chipperfield, Ferruccio Laviani has created modern interior shop fittings to invigorate the classical setting.

Chipperfield, who has been their long-standing and trusted architect for all their major boutiques around the world. For this project, Chipperfield stabilized the historic structure and undertook a 'soft restoration', gently retouching the original colours of the painted ceilings, repairing the plaster cornices and mouldings, bringing back the beauty of the herringbone-patterned parquet flooring. And then, minimalist master that he is, Chipperfield added his signature floors and a staircase in dark grey basalt stone, from Sicily.

For the interior architecture, Dolce and Gabbana invited Ferruccio Laviani to create their vision of how the palazzo should be presented. "I would like to come into a masculine world," Dolce told Laviani, "to have the impression that it is a man's house, not a boutique. And our man is an art collector."

The palazzo is thus a magnificent residence, Laviani having furnished the three floors with large, comfortable armchairs and sofas, great round tables, old Sicilian jars, fine antique Chinese vases and splendid oil paintings. Continuing the domestic theme, the collection is hung in open wardrobes or on floor-fixed racks ("of manly proportions", observes Laviani), and displayed on highly polished walnut sideboards and chests of drawers. The fireplaces have chunky steel chains hung within their openings. Overhead are oversized chandeliers, specially commissioned, in jet-black Murano glass.

For Dolce & Gabbana's flagship store, set in a late eighteenth-century Milanese palazzo, David Chipperfield designed a minimalist staircase in basalt stone. **Left** Traditional elegance in the barber's shop, with chairs covered in custom-made leather upholstery. **Below** The men's grooming salon in white Carrara marble.

Dolce also told Laviani that he wanted "something like in the piazza back in Sicily." So in the area of the former stables of the palazzo, Laviani created a trio of shops on the inner court. There is a grooming salon, in a brilliant white Carrara marble, and the old barber's, in green marble, with a couple of traditional chairs made in Sicily – the manufacturer custom-upgraded them with luxury leather upholstery. And what Italian square is complete without its slice of *dolce vita*? In collaboration with Martini & Rossi, Laviani designed a striking circular bar in the black, red and white of the Martini logo. Two pairs of black marble columns rise from the black Zimbabwean marble mosaic floor, which is inset with a fiery red Chinese dragon. Above, the Murano glass chandelier is a burst of trumpet-shaped cones, "like Martini glasses filled with Martini Rossi," explains its designer.

And look, isn't that Burt Lancaster over there in the corner, sipping a bianco on the rocks?

Opposite The Martini & Rossi bar in the Dolce & Gabbana Milan boutique is done out in the black, red and white of the Martini label; inset in the marble floor is a Chinese dragon.
Above Ferruccio Laviani's Murano glass chandelier is made of trumpet-shaped stems that resemble Martini glasses.
Right The bar's contrast of light and darkness imparts a mood of seduction.

Gianfranco Ferré

via Sant'Andrea
Milan

Gianfranco Ferré / Michael Gabellini

Gianfranco Ferré is a major fashion designer, and an architect. A unique combination. As you would expect, there is an intimate parallel between Ferré's fashion sense and his architecture, especially well illustrated in this boutique. The clothes he designs, it is often remarked, are spectacular, full of glamour, voluminous, opulent, saturated with colour, created for strong and extremely rich women. And here we have his boutique: elegant and luxurious, constructed like one of his ballgowns, impeccably detailed and cut. "To me," Ferré reflects, "architecture is just as much about magic, poetry, dreams and creative flair as fashion is."

The Gianfranco Ferré boutique in Milan occupies a delightful old palazzo. Ferré worked in association with Michael Gabellini, the architect of so many other fine boutiques, as well as with his own in-house architect Ezio Riva. "It was an enmeshed collaboration," observes Gabellini. The full collection is on display in the boutique, women's and men's. And, there is a spa.

The luxury of the Ferré boutique is effusive yet pure; a combination of rich materials and colouring within a design of modern lines and spaces. There is almost something Parisian Art Deco about it, like an exotic room furnished by Jacques-Emile Ruhlmann. Ferré says that, throughout his career, his strongest architectural influence has been the architect Ludwig Mies van der Rohe, who created beauty through the

Above A display cabinet, resembling a travelling trunk and opened to reveal its treasure of Gianfranco Ferré accessories, stands beside the 'floating' red staircase. **Opposite** Views are angled to catch glimpses of the private garden of the palazzo that the boutique occupies. The walls are covered in the reds of waxed stucco, silk shantung and leather.

Being both an architect and a couturier, Gianfranco Ferré is able to harmonize perfectly boutiques and fashion collections. His interiors and clothes are both opulent and luxurious, of exotic and rich materials.

precision of simple spaces and the use of marble, glass, steel and leather, materials that imparted a sense of luxury. "Important, precious hallmarks that express a concept of luxury that is completely free of any exaggeration," Ferré remarks of Mies, although the fashion designer could be commenting upon his own architecture and couture.

On the ground floor of the boutique, the pretty garden behind the palazzo appears around every corner you turn, seen through sheet-glass windows framed in black reflective glass. This sense of edging, which frames and separates and gives intimacy, is felt throughout the boutique: black borders surround doors, screens, furniture, binding the sequence of rooms. The dark tone is

set against the deep red of the walls, an effect like the high-sheen surfaces of Japanese lacquered furniture. Some of the wall surfaces are coloured red in waxed stucco, as is the ceiling on the ground floor; the walls in the women's section are covered in saturated scarlet silk shantung, in the men's zone in red leather, as in a gentleman's club.

The woods are deeply patterned and grained, lights against darks: briar and rosewood for the inset display units, sliding panels in zebrawood and mahogany, Brazilian rosewood and walnut burl. There are crystal and amber insets, mother-of-pearl trays for showing off precious accessories. Shelves are covered in calfskin, goatskin, hand wrinkled using old leather-making techniques. Screens are

of transparent mica, as if taken out of ancient Pompeian windows. The staircase appears to be on fire, a flaming ruby placed within a glass box; it is made of sparkling red fibreglass, while its steel structure is covered in rouged carpeting.

The sense of luxury and opulent use of materials continues in the integral E'spa health spa. The Turkish bath glitters like the sun off a summer lake, its surfaces of dark Bisazza glass mosaic offset by gold. Light splinters from the large mirror-ball sculpture. Slabs of Portoro marble line the walls. And finally, restfully, by the windows overlooking the garden, are terrazzo chaises longues covered in soft, peaceful mattress-cushions.

Above The soothing luxury of a spa chaise longue in the E'spa at the Gianfranco Ferré Milan boutique. **Right** The Turkish bath in Bisazza glass mosaic with its dazzling golden sphere.

Giorgio Armani

via Sant'Andrea
Milan

Claudio Silvestrin

You cannot get much more minimal than the Giorgio Armani boutiques designed by the architect Claudio Silvestrin. One type of stone, one type of wood, clean hard edges, no added colour, no decoration. Yet the architectural statement, and by implication the fashion edict, equals rich and exclusive. Here we have a definite case of that modern axiom, 'less is more'. The lavish use of gold and glitz once stood for the epitome of luxury – and for many people it still does – but the world has turned such standards on its head and now considers the barest of austerities as opulent. But, of course, there is beauty in the naked, although more often than not, most nakedness is not a pretty sight. And so it is

with minimalism: once architecture is stripped of all essentials, there can be no blemishes or anything out of place.

Silvestrin is acknowledged as one of the masters of minimalism. His design for the Giorgio Armani in Milan is another of his many essays in creating a boutique brand look for the fashion designer whose empire has spread around the world, from Beijing to Moscow, São Paulo to Shanghai. The Milan boutique is one of the finest, in the city where Giorgio Armani lives, works and opened his very first shop in 1981.

The Silvestrin boutiques are for Armani's most expensive label. "It's like a club," explains the architect, "exclusive, not flashy, understated,

GIORGIO ARMANI

Left The boutique entrance seen from the street: a thin wall abuts the glass façade, dividing the entrance corridor from the dramatic staircase and display ramp. **Above** The metal ramp, set at an incline, is a slice of architectural theatricality. **Opposite, clockwise from top left** A Giorgio Armani outfit stands in the window against a spectacular backdrop; minimal fixtures and furnishings; a low black ebony bench for displaying accessories skirts the length of the entrance corridor; the entrance with its sunken pool.

Claudio Silvestrin's architecture for Giorgio Armani is almost monastic, and certainly minimal, such as in the sculptural basin of the all-stone washroom (right, above and below). Fittings and fixtures are thin and elongated, with the counters containing sunken display openings (opposite, bottom).

already known by the clients." Thus the architect felt no need to make an aggressive statement to draw in the crowds. Yet the frontage on via Sant'Andrea still attracts the curious with what Silvestrin calls his 'architectural gesture': a long view of a thin slice through the whole length of the building, dramatically emphasized by falling away in a funnel effect. From the street, behind the glass wall, drops an unusable metal ramp, a polished slide; on the far side is its echo, a descending stone staircase. It is like discovering the secret passageway of an ancient Egyptian pyramid, with the slide being the trick entry to catch tomb raiders off guard.

The real entrance to the boutique, to the left, is quietly inviting. The lobby gives on to a shallow pool, its still waters on a plane with the floor. All is in warm cappuccino-coloured Saint-Maximin stone, used throughout for floors and walls. A long corridor, parallel to and on the other side of the drop-away feature, leads to the principal ground-floor sales area. A low bench, 40 m (130 ft) long, stretches its length, dotted with shoes and accessories. It is made of black Macassar ebony, a rich material that is used throughout for all the furniture.

The collection is set out on a grid, a place to be explored: in and about the great stone partition walls, around the display tables and along lines of clothing. With such minimal interior design, the clothes show to great advantage, finely lit by the long rows of little square lights and hidden illuminators.

There is undoubtedly something monastic about the whole experience of Silvestrin's Giorgio Armani boutiques. The architect admits to a deep admiration for the Romanesque style, especially of Cistercian architecture. It makes you wonder if that little water feature at the entrance to the boutique might not be an Early Christian full-immersion baptismal pool.

Miss Sixty

Via Montenapoleone
Milan

Studio 63 Architecture and Design

Do you recall the 1968 cult science fiction film *Barbarella*, starring the voluptuous young Jane Fonda rolling around in her shag pile carpeted spacecraft? "Baa Baa Baa Barbarella, Barbarella psychedella," went the wonderfully inane lyrics, "Dazzle me with rainbow colours." If you don't remember it, then you probably shop at a Miss Sixty boutique.

Because the main clientele for Miss Sixty are young women, born well after 1968. They're hip, they're sassy, they're casual glam – like the clothes, like the boutiques. The style of the Miss Sixty collection is touched by the 1960s and '70s: short skirts, spiky heels, hip-hugging jeans. The designer and co-founder of Miss Sixty is Wichy Hassan, who has built this retro chic look into a small empire. There are Miss Sixty shops worldwide, from Chile to Macedonia. And to these Hassan has added Energie boutiques, carrying his label for young men.

Dropping this Miss Sixty boutique right on the venerable high-fashion street of via Montenapoleone is almost an act of rebellion. It's like putting a mini-skirt on your granny. The neighbours are aristocratic and this looks like just a bit of fun. But you have to be careful, because it is all too easy to dismiss this boutique as a piece of kitsch camp, a quirky bit of Groovy Revival. Actually, this is sophisticated Modern Retro by a team of architects who understand mid-twentieth-century design as well as Robert Adam in the eighteenth century understood and then reinterpreted ancient Roman architecture and decoration for wealthy Brits.

From their Florence room with a view of the Ponte Vecchio, architects Piero Angelo Orecchioni and Massimo Dei of Studio 63 oversee the design of the Miss Sixty and Energie boutiques. They are the same age as Wichy Hassan, born in the early 1960s, and click right into his revivalist concept. Each of their Miss Sixty boutiques is different, attempting to relate to the city it inhabits. "The language is the same, but the words are

Shaggy white carpets undulate against the gloss of the yellow floors and walls. The graphics are large and bold. The pop psychedelia of the design catches the vibrancy of Miss Sixty's youthful clients.

Opposite A backdrop of rounded wooden baubles hangs
behind Miss Sixty Milan's shoe display and alongside the
staircase with its white carpeted walls. **Below** A pair of
Arne Jacobsen-designed chairs on the mezzanine level,
in front of the chain chandeliers.

different," says Tami Eyal, the spokeswoman for
the Italian team. "We aim to take a source of
inspiration from the city, what is behind the city,"
she continues. And then they marry it up with
the Miss Sixty collection.

In Milan, they got it spot on, capturing the
expensive pedigree of the street. Here they struck
out to make the boutique feel opulent. It certainly
feels golden. The walls, floors and display units
are in a rich yellow. And like Barbarella's spaceship,
there is a lot of white shag, or to use its more
Continental nomenclature, moquette. It crawls
over the surfaces, undulating around the mirrored
stainless steel columns, up the walls, wrapping

around the display shelves. Everything has
rounded edges, a well-loved configuration of
the 1960s. "There is movement, femininity,
no hard lines," points out Eyal.

As a Modern Retro interior, it mixes vintage
with new. The wire-steel framed chairs and tables,
like closely strung harps, were designed by
Warren Platner in 1966 and there are pairs of
Arne Jacobsen's Swan chairs. The chandeliers,
made of long chains, are by Studio 63, as are
the lighting fixtures designed in the form of
stamens bursting from the centre of petals
etched in mirror glass. Flower power?

Below Miss Sixty Milan's Modern Retro look is reinforced by the steel-wire framed stool and chair by Warren Platner in the dressing room and seating area. **Opposite** Flower power in etched glass, with stamens of light.

Moschino

via Sant'Andrea
Milan

Sean Dix

'Caveat emptor' reads the Latin motto printed on the lampshades overhanging the buyer tables in the Moschino private showrooms in Milan. Translation: 'Let the buyer beware'.

The designer of the showroom, Sean Dix, clearly knew how to capture the irreverent spirit of the fashion house of Moschino. So much so that the company asked him back to design several of their Milan boutiques. This one in via Sant'Andrea is similar to, but a little more opulent than, the other just around the corner in via della Spiga. These are boutiques with humour, gently mocking (but not blaspheming) the fashion industry, the customer and even the company itself. It is, you might say, a case of tongue in chic.

It was the late Franco Moschino, who died in 1994 at only forty-four years of age, who established this satirical sartorial direction. In 1982, he had launched his first collection with such legendary slogans as 'Fashion is a waist of money' stitched into the clothes. Later he was sued by the House of Chanel for making a joke at the expense of their famous perfume, on a T-shirt illustrated with a television set and the message 'Channel No. 5'.

The witty effects of Dix's boutique design are subtle, carried out with such style that the messages are almost subliminal. "Some people notice them, others don't," Dix observes with amusement. "That's the fun of it." Trotting past the shop windows, you cannot help but catch sight of the pretty chandeliers. But stop, and you realize that they are composed of tinkling cascades of clear shoes: Cinderella's glass slipper. Each, and there are ninety per chandelier, was hand-blown by a woman glassmaker who usually crafts fancy Grappa bottles.

The fairy tales, and fashion encoding, continues. Along the 15 m (50 ft) wall is the text, in English and Italian, of Hans Christian Andersen's tale 'The Emperor's New Clothes'. "'But the Emperor has nothing at all on!' said a little child." And like the silly emperor who listened to his

This Moschino boutique is brimming with the irreverent wit and humour of its late founder. The Cinderella glass slipper chandelier (above), designed by Sean Dix, hangs alongside a wall printed with the text of the fairy tale 'The Emperor's New Clothes'.

courtiers (or should that be 'couturiers'?), the text wall is showing everything and nothing – white lettering which drops a shadowing upon a fabric ecru background. There, but not there.

Near the centre of the shop, a great pile of material holds up the ceiling. At least, that's the way it seems. This is another example, like the slipper chandelier, says Dix, of using "materials from fashion in architectural ways, and *vice versa*." The pile, which hides the existing support column, is made of stacked fabric – one on top of another, and another, and another, nearly 40 km (25 miles) worth of it (well, that's the claim) in three shades of brilliant red. The other column is textured with dressmaking pins, from top to bottom, squillions of them.

There is more fabric stacking for the seating, and for the long bench near the accessories, and for the stools in the changing rooms. The only non-Dix piece is the 'cross-check' armchair by Frank Gehry, ribbons of bentwood that Dix felt fitted the ethos of his allegory.

The table display units, too, are what they aren't: large eighteenth-century commodes in rich-grained woods are but life-size photographic reproductions, applied to the mirror surfaces of polished stainless steel.

At the rear of the boutique is a backlit wall, one section of panels laser-cut to simulate lace and the other of white back-painted glass that shines, laughs Dix, "like glossy nail polish".

At Moschino Milan, Sean Dix has used a theme of fashion materials: some walls are studded with dressing pins, seating is made of piled fabrics, hanging lamps are of wound string, illuminated screens feature lacy perforation.

Paul Smith

via Manzoni
Milan

Sophie Hicks

"The key to the design," says Sophie Hicks, architect of Paul Smith's boutique in Milan, "is the two major display tables." The one down the centre of the principal space is a long, old carpenter's table, complete with metal vice, which Paul Smith found in Tuscany. Over one end of it, Hicks has placed a glass 'bridge', a raised shelf. The other display unit, near the entrance, is a wooden six-legged dining-room table, with bulbous turned legs. "When we found it, there were only the rounded ends, the middle leaf was missing. So we joined the ends together by inserting a set of glass drawers for displaying jewellery. We didn't try to make the display tables look new, we just transformed them."

Vintage with contemporary, traditional with modern, a little this with a little that: that's the Paul Smith style. His clothing collections mix cool–clean–classic and coloured–patterned–complex. And the effect always hints at something very British, a look that is particularly popular in Japan, where Paul Smith has more than two hundred of his 225 or so shops and concessions.

He opened his first shop in Nottingham in 1970. But it was his 1979 Floral Street boutique in London's then hot new shopping area of Covent Garden that made such an impact. It looked, as it still does, like a gentleman's outfitters, with rich wooden counters and shelving; but placed throughout are vintage and modern pictures

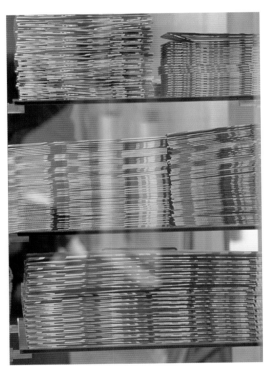

Left The entrance space with the old dining table that was transformed into a display table by Sophie Hicks. The architect enjoys mixing vintage with new in a very relaxed manner. **Above** The distinctive striped packaging of Paul Smith. **Opposite** The boutique is formed out of the courtyard of an eighteenth-century palazzo. The walls have been washed pink and vintage pieces introduced, like the old carpenter's table.

and furniture, tin toys and teddy bears, an ever-changing fun arcade of market-stall buys and cutting-edge artefacts.

Sir Paul laments the state of boutiques at present. "Although much of the world is very well informed," he says, "although communication is better than ever and although people have never travelled so far and so often, I'm disappointed at the homogeneity of shops around the world. The interior design is similar, fashions are similar."

But certainly not his shops. "He's brimming over with hundreds of ideas for his boutiques," laughs Sophie Hicks, "and it is up to me to know what to leave out." Hicks and Smith first worked together in 1998 on the very successful (both for design and sales) Paul Smith shop-in-a-house in London's Notting Hill. "It was a happy start," recalls Hicks, a fashion-savvy architect who took up the profession after spending a decade in fashion publishing, first as fashion editor of *Tatler* magazine, then British *Vogue*. She's seen a few boutiques in her time.

The Paul Smith boutique in Milan is part of a large eighteenth-century townhouse, the Palazzo Gallarati Scotti, across the busy via Manzoni from the Armani Centre (see page 52). And you couldn't get a greater contrast in boutique styles. Whereas Michael Gabellini's large emporium for Armani is about exquisite detailing, a cool palette and sophisticated spaces, Hicks's boutique is a jolly hothouse hybrid.

For a start, and this you certainly can't miss, it is all plastered in a vivid pink. Carpets are large square swatches of different colours. An expansive yellow painting by the artist Richard Woods hangs over the principal space. The speckled terrazzo floor has coral-pink edging dividing the original from Hicks's new sections. Pink crushed velvet curtains hang behind the ladies' lingerie section, and the same material covers the handrail of the pretty cast-iron staircase.

With its narrow round-headed arches, old furniture and glass shelves scattered with *objets trouvés*, the boutique has a rawness about it, of something found, played with … and definitely transformed.

Piombo

via della Spiga
Milan

Ferruccio Laviani

Brass is a metal that has a very small place in the high fashion boutique interior. Stainless steel, yes – brass, no. With all its associations with hard, mirrory Modernism, stainless steel is the preferred metal of today. Brass is considered by many designers to be too malleable, and as antiquated as brass candlesticks. Yet, here it is, used throughout the Piombo boutique in Milan, and with polished sophistication.

Even the architect, Ferruccio Laviani, admits that brass is a difficult material to use. But it does have, he says, its glamour (another rather retro word) and was a popular material in post-war design, especially in France and Italy. Laviani has used many references and vintage pieces from the 1950s in his design for this boutique, and as brass is the only, and therefore thematic, metal throughout, it carries the connotation of a period of great elegance in Italian interiors.

Fashion tailor Massimo Piombo sought out this look of historical continuity from Laviani, asking the architect to create a boutique modelled on those ateliers from the past when fashion was very much still a tailoring craft. The outcome is rather like an updated tailors from London's Savile Row. Piombo's collections of men's wear, his suits and jackets, are always gentlemanly, exquisitely cut, rich in textured fabrics. Boutique and attire have thus found their complements.

Piombo and Laviani inherited the building space on via della Spiga as a jumble of small rooms on different levels. But they liked the idea of compartments, of discovery, of moving from room to room. The rooms were, recalls Laviani, "the soul of the space." They were kept as such, but totally redesigned as a selection of salons, each reflecting the collection contents. The building's envelope was revealed, with walls taken right back to the concrete, and the floor made to match. "I wanted the precious inside the non-precious," comments the architect, "like a diamond in the rough."

Ferruccio Laviani cleverly used unfashionable brass throughout the Piombo boutique, as trim on the furniture, for the clothing rails and lighting fixtures. The luminous yellow of the furnishings is offset against the raw concrete walls.

The entrance to the Piombo boutique is along a cut-through between buildings, a long outdoor room. The visitor enters on a level overlooking the main room of the boutique. Against the grey of the floor and walls stands the delightful shock of the canary-yellow furnishings; sitting upon the large yellow carpet are yellow armchairs and sofas trimmed in polished brass, all designed by Laviani. Suits from the City range hang within this carpeted zone, upon prominent freestanding rails – brass, of course. The brass chandeliers overhead, part of a series throughout the boutique, are fine vintage pieces, designed in 1959 by Gino Sarfatti for Arteluce. Large wardrobes of dark chestnut line the wall.

The next room is around the corner. It is subdivided by a red laminated plastic screen edged in polished brass with more clothing rails attached. On one side is another quiet sitting area, with a set of Margherita chairs designed by Franco Albini, classics from the 1950s, made in rattan, this pair in a lacquered Chinese red. The floor lamp, made of tubular brass that splays out to take the light, was made by Flos to Laviani's design. The section on the other side is called the Garden Room, its ceiling of curving glazed panels pierced by the trunk of a tree rising from the floor.

Beyond are a series of cave-like spaces with roughly vaulted ceilings. One room has a touch of the exotic: its end wall is dominated by a luxurious panel of lapis lazuli, with brass inlay lettering, in Arabic, spelling out Massimo Piombo's name; while the long wall is of pierced brass panels, like a modern version of screens from a Moorish palace. Another room, the Party Room, is for evening wear and has mirrors with engraved patterns of diamond shapes. Indeed, diamonds in the rough.

Left The Piombo Milan boutique is created from a series of rooms, many of them with their walls finished in unpainted concrete.
Below A small vaulted salon with a lapis lazuli panel at one end and a brass standing lamp designed by Ferruccio Laviani.

Above The Piombo Party Room with evening dress. **Opposite** The trunk of a living tree pierces the Garden Room's glass roof.

NEW YORK

Alexander McQueen

William Russell

Carlos Miele

Asymptote

Donna Karan New York

Enrico Bonetti and Dominic Kozerski

Issey Miyake Tribeca

Frank Gehry/G TECTS LLC: Gordon Kipping

Prada Epicenter

Rem Koolhaas/Office for Metropolitan Architecture (OMA)

Stella McCartney

Universal Design Studio

Alexander McQueen

West 14th Street
New York

William Russell

The 'bad boy of fashion' has grown up. Everyone agrees. Alexander McQueen is still very young in the world of high fashion; he was born in 1970. Yet these past few years have seen him shed his wild anti-establishment views and mature not only as a designer, but also into a man with a sharp business sense. His transformation was quick, from the rough streets of London's East End, graduating from St Martins College, taken up as chief designer for the French couture house Givenchy, then going solo, all in less time, so it seems, than it takes to slip into one of his famous low-cut 'bumsters'.

A sure sign of McQueen's coming of age has been the opening of a string of his own-label boutiques. And they're cool. And sleek. And, well, still a little bit bad-boy. The first opened in Tokyo, and then this one in New York, then the next in London, then Milan, then … the world is for conquering.

McQueen chose his friend William Russell to be his architect. They created the look of the boutiques as if they were a duo designing the next fall–winter collection. As a starter, they collected images, then tacked them up on a pinboard, kept rearranging them into a collage, and thus slowly synthesized the essence of the design. What they discovered was that they wanted something eclectic, organic in form, curvaceous.

The result is a boutique where the forms never seem to stand still. The space is rounded and white, like a series of igloos, with walls glowing with the light of the midnight Arctic sun. During one fashion season, a large portrait image of an Inuit hunter, in his hooded parka, gazed over the boutique from the backlit light box near the entrance. That certainly was a man who looked at home.

The white-plastered side walls, inset with rails for clothing, gracefully curve at the bottom to meet the terrazzo floors. Hanging from the ceiling, like icicles, are the display units. These arch at the ceiling to give the whole boutique the feel of

Opposite, top A sweeping canopy over the street entrance. **Opposite, bottom** Structural columns are cloaked with mirrors and display shelves. **This page** In an interior that is sleek, curvaceous, white and as cool as an igloo, McQueen's colourful collection stands out. A touch of pattern in the etched glass of the suspended display case reflects the luxury of the designer's embroideries and accessories.

being built in the vaults of a glacial cathedral. Some of the units, made of sheet aluminium on frames, do not touch the floor but are suspended to give an uninterrupted effect at foot level. Many of the cut-outs for shelving have curved outlines of varied shapes; some are pierced straight through so that display objects can been seen on all sides. One of the 'icicles' ends in a glass and mirrored display case etched in a florid Victorian pattern.

At the centre of the boutique is what the designer and his architect jokingly call the 'mother ship': an oval form containing three internal fitting rooms decked out in walnut. Partially encircling this large form is a suspended clothes rail.

Like the floor, the serving desks, counter and seating shelf at the rear of the boutique are made of terrazzo. Although the stone is dark in colour, it is highlighted with chips of sparkling white mother-of-pearl.

Structural piers are wrapped in mirrors. All the light fixtures are partially concealed so that the open shelving radiates light. The principal illumination meanders throughout the whole boutique, inset in flush bands just above the underside of the suspended units. The lighting is thus integrated right into the form, part of the attempt by the architect to "dissolve the legibility of the building so as to accentuate the ethereality of the space".

Carlos Miele

West 14th Street
New York

Asymptote

Hot designer, hot architects, cool interior. Carlos Miele is Brazil's most famous fashion designer. Asymptote are a husband-and-wife team of architects who push the limits of fluidity through space, their boutique like white-crested waves rolling on to Copacabana Beach.

Hani Rashid and Lise Anne Couture (a surname surreally appropriate for this project) are Asymptote, important movers and shakers of the exploration into digitally designed architecture – digi-architecture. Their research comes to life in the Carlos Miele boutique; you have the feeling of being inside a computer-generated design. The space is continuous, sinuous and slick, as if it has slipped off the screen into white reality.

The liquidity of the interior was developed through computer studies by the architects starting from scraps of fabric from Miele's design studio. The idea was to "structure pattern for space the way pattern is structured for body," says Rashid. The surfaces are plywood, bent and lacquered. And, to borrow a term from the client's world, seamless. The glistening epoxy surfaces of floor, walls and high-gloss PVC ceiling blend into one another. Openings are sculpted: sloping holes and slanting sides like the piercings in a Barbara Hepworth sculpture. You can sense the computer mouse as it slithers around the architects' screen.

Down the centre of the space, the cut-out wall cloaks the structural columns, while the undulating platforms here and around the perimeter walls serve to display items and create seating. The clothes are set and hung on the outer edges in illuminated enclosures. But the most spectacular intercessions are the mannequins placed in the open spaces, suspended on near-invisible steel wires and hovering over glass rings of embedded neon and halogen lighting set in the floor.

The circles of light are echoed in the two art installations. The first, near the entrance, is

a video image of a shadowy figure, made difficult to read by the reflections off the dark mirrored glass. The second, near the rear of the boutique, is much livelier, a great circular concave mirror on to which are projected moving images of fire and water. Both works are a collaboration between Asymptote and Carlos Miele, a designer who not only experiments with fabric, but also creates shows of video and dance performance in many major galleries.

Miele is passionate about his native Brazil, and uses the colour, vibrancy and materials of his country in his fashion designs. He has more than sixty shops in Brazil, but his New York boutique is his first outside the country. A man with a social conscience, he has used his professional influence to develop native artisan handiwork, employing the skills of seamstresses and lacemakers in the slum *favalas*, and even commissioning the indigenous Amazonian feather art of *plumária*. One critic, with cheeky reverence, has labelled Miele's style 'samba school evening wear'. In the white atmosphere of the Asymptote boutique, it shows to perfection.

Previous pages A mannequin seems to hover over a circle of light in Carlos Miele New York's sculpted interior, which belies the highly computer-generated design. **Below** It is as if the heat of the Brazilian fashion designer's collection has melted the space. **Opposite** Collection pieces are hung along perimeter walls, leaving the central spaces for individual display, seating and fashion-show walks.

Donna Karan New York

Madison Avenue
New York

Enrico Bonetti and Dominic Kozerski

As soon as you step over the threshold of this spacious three-storeyed boutique, you have the perception of being enveloped in a Zen-like experience. Almost all the senses pulse, but slowly, gently, quietly. Visually, the eye is released into a space that flows on and out. Audibly, the ear is soothed by the tranquil sounds wafting through the music system. And your sense of smell is warmly awoken by the aromas of essential oils released through the air conditioning.

Donna Karan is America's premier female fashion designer, the most widely known and, financially, the most successful. Yet her style is restrained, classic, everywoman. You cannot get simpler than one of her characteristic outfits: a blouse or T-shirt, skirt or trousers, and a jacket. In her collections, as here in her Madison Avenue boutique, she seeks, through simplicity, to evoke a spiritual awakening within her clients. There is that fun and sporty side to her, which she lets loose in her DKNY label and whizzy DKNY shops. But with her luxury Donna Karan New York brand, she seems to come closer to her true self.

Donna Karan and her architects, the Italian Enrico Bonetti and the Englishman Dominic Kozerski, found their starting point for the new boutique on a day in London, when the three of them visited an exhibition at the Saatchi Gallery. Filling one whole room was but one large installation. Called 20:50, by the artist Richard

Clockwise from above left The large and expansive showcase for the Donna Karan New York brand; a view into the atrium, with its pool edging and glass wall to the central courtyard; a bench by Zaha Hadid snakes through the space.
Opposite Beneath the staircase, a display screen evokes hearth and home.

Wilson, it was formed of a pool of smooth, dark and reflective sump oil. Here the trio discovered the "black of infinite depth", recalls Kozerski, a concept of space that never stops and yet always returns.

So, the question became: how to translate this impression of a secret infinity to within a late nineteenth-century New York building, one originally designed by the Beaux-Arts architects Carrère & Hastings? The key was found in creating a large inner courtyard as the focal area, a point which the customer circulates around, leaves, returns to. Climbing the full height of the shop, the back wall is glazed, with views of the patterned brick of the surrounding buildings. The ground floor is a garden, edged with a black pool reminiscent of the Wilson installation. Its dark water is carried beneath the internal glass wall, taking the inside out and bringing the outside in.

The courtyard flooring is Portland stone imported from England, and this is the principal material used throughout the store. Two rough stone sculptures by Izumi Masatoshi are placed on the patio, beneath a towering thicket of bamboo. Stepping into this atrium garden, over the pool, the visitor is reflected in a large mirror that leans against the far wall.

The reverberations continue in the theme of reflective black. Near the entrance is a great black wall, the background for the mannequin displays. The merchandise on the ground floor, for home and lifestyle, is set on dark mahogany shelving within black niches. The display furnishings, tables and fixtures are in reclaimed Bali teak.

The stone and glass central staircase is dramatic. Set at an angle to the entrance, it switches more than 90 degrees at the first-floor level to the men's section, rising to the women's on the second. Here on the top floor are two principal spaces. At the rear is a room with a bay window overlooking the internal garden. At the front is the *salon*, with the original glass doors leading to the over-street terrace, screened with translucent silk. But contrasting darkness returns with the zigzag bench down the centre, a black glossy sculpture by the architect Zaha Hadid. Glowing in the traditional fireplace are flames that waver over a bed of black river rocks. Here is our destination – home, to peace and tranquility.

Opposite The naturalness of wood and stone enforces the spiritual simplicity of Donna Karan's collection. **Above** Internal windows overlook the atrium.

Issey Miyake Tribeca

Hudson Street
New York

Frank Gehry/
G TECTS LLC: Gordon Kipping

Blustering, billowing, bending and rolling – *Tornado* is the appropriately named 7.5 m (25 ft) sculpture twirling its way through this boutique. Caught up in this twister, however, Dorothy and Toto would not end up in the Land of Oz but rather in the heart of New York's Tribeca. And here there are certainly none of those grubby little Munchkins. The population is made up of chic mannequins hugged up in Issey Miyake textiles.

The sculpture is by Frank Gehry, and its undulating form and gleaming surface of polished titanium is reminiscent of the architect's most famous building, the Guggenheim Museum in Bilbao, Spain. It also carries overtones of Issey Miyake's fashion designs, celebrated for their innovative shapes, flowing line and movement. Here in Hudson Street, Miyake has grouped all his collections, most famously his Pleats Please: clothes that are pleated, cut, sewn then pressed to form permanent wrinkly crinkles; and his A-POC line: outfits cut from a single tubular piece of material and customized to fit the owner. The beauty of Miyake's clothing can be astonishing.

The boutique occupies but a small area of the whole Issey Miyake flagship building. The retail space on two of the three floors is nestled in among administrative offices, a showroom, a press area and stockrooms unseen by the public, and takes up only a fifth of the 1400 sq. m (15,000 sq ft) total. The whole edifice, the Spice Building, was once a warehouse, designed in 1888 in a rather placid red brick that masks a wonderful cast-iron structure full of fancy trimmings of columns and decoration. It is rumoured that the cost of conversion was $4,000,000.

The project architect was the Canadian Gordon Kipping, the Toronto-born architect now based in Manhattan, a teaching colleague at Columbia University of Frank Gehry, who was also born in Toronto. Kipping, who calls his firm G TECTS LLC, has woven his design around *Tornado* while revealing parts of the building's historic fabric. Especially accentuated are the timber beams of

Below The rugged old cast-iron grilling and pilasters at the entrance of the boutique frame the slick modern titanium of Frank Gehry's sculpture inside. **Opposite** The folding and crumpling of the metal surfaces evokes the innovative pleating and cutting of textiles by Issey Miyake.

the ceilings. On the ground floor, the linear pattern, colouring and texture of the wood contrast with the undulating silvery metal of the sculpture.

Edging the ground-floor space is a wide band of glass sunk into the flooring. Through it are revealed the timber beams beneath, plus the goings-on down on the lower ground floor of the boutique. The glass is patterned in alternating frosted and clear diagonal stripes, continuing the effect of movement that is also carried into the jagged edging of the perfume showcase behind the service counter.

The metal-sided cave of the ground floor gives way on the level below to Kipping's glass-walled room, which anchors the centre of the space. Practically, the enclosed area is isolated from the working spaces around, making it secure. Aesthetically, it affords an aura of exclusivity. Clothes hang from stainless steel racks with large pneumatically driven wheels, a high-class joke on the ubiquitous racks seen daily bumping along the pavements of New York's rag-trade district.

Left Frank Gehry's *Tornado* rips through the Issey Miyake New York boutique beneath the exposed wooden beams of the former warehouse's ceilings. **Above** Tranquility is to be found in the glass-walled room on the lower level.

Prada Epicenter

Broadway at Prince Street
New York

Rem Koolhaas/Office for Metropolitan Architecture (OMA)

Come and worship at the altar of the golden goddess of boutiques, the collaboration of cult architect Rem Koolhaas and fashion priestess Miuccia Prada. Here our goddess, in the human guise of consumer entertainment, has descended in all her glory.

But do we believe in this goddess? As in all matters of religion, there are true believers and those who doubt. Judging by the number of visitors and tourists who make a pilgrimage to this boutique simply because of its reputation, the SoHo Prada is an overwhelming success. However, it has its critics, those who question whether the innovative features are successful. Either way, this is a shopping space of great sanctity.

This is certainly not one of Prada's familiar mint-green boutiques. Rem Koolhaas has impressed his own mark quite firmly here in a design that is daring, experimental and flexible. You can almost smell the theoretical origins of the building, backed by work that Koolhaas and his students published in their heavy volume *Harvard Design School guide to shopping*.

The ground-floor façade on Broadway has one of those delicate openings local to the area, edged in Victorian cast iron. The interior, therefore, comes as a surprise, for instead of the expected little boutique, the space is expansive – 2100 sq. m (23,000 sq ft) – narrow but deep, reaching through the depth of the city block to within sight of

Opposite, far left Above 'the wave' of the principal space is the 'hanging city', a series of moveable cages for art installations and display. **Opposite, left** two views of the circular glass lift. **Far left** Zebrawood stairs inset into 'the wave'. **Left** A caged mannequin riding the crest of 'the wave'. **Below** The semi-opaque polycarbonate-panelled wall with an entrance to the room where merchandise is displayed, below street level.

Steps down one side of the New York Prada Epicenter 'wave' double as display ledges, as here with a small army of Prada-clad mannequins, and also as seating for performances and fashion shows. The expansive billboard wall features a changing presentation of decorative murals.

Mercer Street. Near the entrance is a cylindrical lift, in effect a small room 3.6m (12 ft) in diameter, displaying shoes and accessories as well as carrying passengers up and down one storey. Running the length of one of the side walls of the main space is an enormous graphic billboard, or 'wallpaper', a changeable work of art. The side opposite, backing Prince Street, is luminous and semi-opaque, consisting of panels of polycarbonate covering the brick wall and windows.

The great architectural feature of the interior is 'the wave', a continuation of the zebrawood flooring at the entrance that dips to the lower level and then rises back to ground level. The side closest to Broadway is stepped, doubling

as display shelving and, during performances or fashion shows, as audience seating similar to that in ancient Greek and Roman theatres. The smooth surface opposite conceals an events platform that can be mechanically unfolded.

Overhead, and in the far end display area, are cages that look as if they were made for bungee jumpers to ascend in. Dubbed 'hanging city' by the architect, these cages display mannequins and merchandise, and run along motorized tracks in the ceiling.

Perversely, the sales areas of the Prada Epicenter are pushed, some might say squeezed, to either side of the lower level in a series of small rooms and corridors. Items are displayed

on shelving set in rows that glide back and forth, like rolling stacks used in libraries that are short of space.

A great deal of research, and expense, went into the new technology of the store. Most popular has proved to be the changing rooms. With a tap on the foot pedal, the sliding doors electro-opaque from translucent to transparent. Unnervingly, like a two-way mirror, the customer's side remains clear. Once changed, by means of a 'magic mirror', the customer can turn and see themselves from behind, revealed sequentially on a video-based screen in a time-delayed playback.

There are three dedicated media booths for audiovisual presentations. And various screens,

The Prada Epicenter in New York has been the most talked-about and visited of all the city's new boutiques. The design by Rem Koolhaas is big and bold, filled with innovative ideas on display, and futurist in its use of technology.

known as 'ubiquitous displays', hang among the clothes and lie on shelves. They look like little art installations, but they play art videos and graphics, and give out merchandise information. When the store first opened, they were linked to the wireless, hand-held devices used by the sales staff, sophisticated controls which transmitted data about in-store inventory and shoppers' personal buying details such as sizes and past purchases. But the hand-helds subsequently proved a disappointment, a case perhaps of over-ambitious technology.

Nevertheless, everyone seems a convert to such an audacious enterprise.

Left A caged Prada collection hovers just off the floor.
Top The rolling stacks of the main collection display units.
Above In the changing room, clients can view themselves in a time-delayed video playback.

Stella McCartney

West 14th Street
New York

Universal Design Studio

"I know what makes a chick tick," says Stella McCartney. And the young fashion designer is not simply talking about her line of ready-to-wear clothes, shoes and accessories. With the first boutique she opened, in New York's meatpacking district, Stella McCartney has begun making women, and a good few men, tick about interior architecture.

The daughter of ex-Beatle Sir Paul and Linda McCartney, Stella has been surrounded by the royalty of pop and entertainment all her life. In 1995, at her graduating show from St Martins College of Art and Design in London, super-models Naomi Campbell and Kate Moss walked down the catwalk wearing her designs. Her rise was meteoric. Two years after her graduation, Stella McCartney had succeeded Karl Lagerfeld as chief designer to the French couture house Chloe. When her close friend Madonna got married in 2000, Stella created the wedding dress.

Stella McCartney's style of fashion is passionately informed by her outlook on life. Her dresses are admired for their figure-hugging qualities that reveal a woman's natural lines; for their use of natural, rich materials such as silk and satin; and for integrating antique buttons and lace. Although she enjoys the fun of artificial materials, McCartney is in accord with the natural world. She is outspoken on her distaste for the use of animal skins. Taking the helm from her late mother, Stella McCartney is a leading advocate for the campaign against the maltreatment of animals. Even leather is abhorrent to her.

McCartney chose Universal Design Studio to bring her natural style into the urban environment of New York. For her shop, Edward Barber and Jay Osgerby, the founders of Universal, transformed a former 370 sq. m (4000 sq ft) warehouse into 'a landscape'. Floors appear to be contoured, water ripples, plant forms wave. Weaving among these forms, the visitor is coaxed into exploring the terrain ... and the collection.

Below Mannequins appear to float above the still waters of a pool running the length of the window display. Stella McCartney seeks harmony through nature in her collection of clothing designs. Her boutique is thus 'a landscape', with its pool, contoured surfaces and environmental-friendly collection with no animal materials. **Opposite** A pair of chairs by Hvidt & Møgaard-Nielsen stand before a curtain of metal rods and ceiling-suspended rails.

The theme of nature at Stella McCartney extends to the walls, which are textured in a cell pattern of ceramic six-petal flowers, and to the rod screens that evoke reeds and grasses.

The first impression of the tranquility of the interior is glimpsed from the street by the passer-by. The line of mannequins in the window hovers above a long dark pool of water, rising like well-dressed inhabitants of Atlantis. Once within, the visitor travels the landscape of the shop by wandering over the terrazzo floor, which is embedded with curving metal lines in the pattern of countour lines on a topographical map. Long 'reeds' or 'grasses' made of pink and ivory metal rods cluster together, swaying as the visitor moves about. Nearby stands a great tree, its branches blossoming with accessories: little silk clutches from the designer's own line, and vintage objects – antique buttons, shoes, even doorknobs.

The walls extend the horizon of nature. The western wall is a tapestry of images – flowers, hummingbirds, a female centaur. These figures are McCartney's own designs, screen-printed on a peach-coloured fabric. Towards the central area, another hummingbird and a dandelion are inlaid into the wood panelling in imitation mother-of-pearl marquetry.

The eastern wall is a representation of the basic building block of nature – the cell. Barber and Osgerby designed the wall in white ceramic tiles, each tile hexagonal, like a honeycomb of a beehive, overlaid with a six-petal flower pattern. This is the microcosm of the harmony of nature, of all design and, by association, of Stella McCartney's fashion collection.

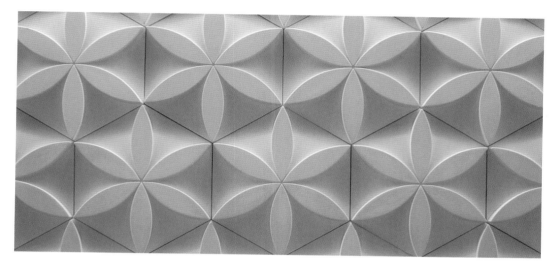

PARIS

Calvin Klein

John Pawson

Chanel

Peter Marino

Comme des Garçons

Takao Kawasaki/Rei Kawakubo/KRD: Shona Kitchen and Abe Rogers

Helmut Lang

Gluckman Mayner

Jean Paul Gaultier

Philippe Starck

John Galliano

Wilmotte Associés: Jean-Michel Wilmotte

Kenzo

Jean-Jacques Ory/DeuxL: Lena Pessoa/Tiziano Vudafieri/Emmanuelle Duplay

Pucci

DeuxL: Lena Pessoa/Tiziano Vudafieri

Calvin Klein

avenue Montaigne
Paris

John Pawson

Purity in clothes and purity in architecture. Calvin Klein and John Pawson were made for each other: the fashion designer who for more than forty years has set the standard for creating clothes of fresh clean lines, and the architect who is the maestro of minimalism. "I have always believed in simplicity," says Klein. "I have never put women into ruffles and fanciful apparel. To me that seems silly."

When Klein opened his New York flagship boutique on Madison Avenue in 1995, his first design venture with Pawson, it was an instant hit. Fashion and architectural critics hailed it as a new breed of boutique, a new approach to interior design, the perfect example of minimalism. There was an feeling of spaciousness, great areas of space sparsely populated with merchandise; large windows uncluttered with displays; simple, natural surfaces treated with obsessive precision. It all had the atmosphere of an art gallery, with the clothes and accessories as display objects.

Pawson's earlier commissions had been for owners of major London art galleries, such as Hester van Royen, Leslie Waddington and Clodagh, doing both their galleries and apartments – just as he was to do Calvin Klein's own apartment too. Display is Pawson's forte, achieved in a setting of pared-down simplicity.

After the Madison Avenue boutique, other Calvin Klein boutiques by Pawson began to open around the world: in Dubai and Hamburg; in Britain's Bluewater shopping mall in Kent; and in Seoul, South Korea, with a freestanding building faced in stone to create an impressive monolith.

The boutique on Paris's avenue Montaigne, the capital's most chic fashion street, comes as the culmination of this symbiotic relationship, as Calvin Klein sold his fashion house soon after the completion of this project. It is, in many ways, a compact edition of the Madison Avenue boutique, showing men's and women's collections as well as homeware. In Europe it is not necessary to have as much display area as in America; Europeans, on the whole, are satisfied with a

Opposite A slice of light draws clients up to the first floor. **Below** John Pawson's architecture is synonymous with the style known as minimalism, and his Calvin Klein boutiques are his best-known works. The designs are sharp, clean and precise; the simplicity is at times so self-effacing that only the merchandise is noticeable.

smaller selection of sizes and colours and will wait while the assistant fetches a greater range from behind the scenes.

The sensation is crisp. Stone floors, white walls, glass shelves. To achieve such simplicity is not easy; detailing and craftsmanship must be outstanding to sustain the aura of elegant exclusivity required for such a luxury boutique.

All the glass of the windows is set flush with the walls. These walls, in turn, are plastered using a special French technique to impart a particularly flat and even surface. Corners are given knife-edge profiles, and made tough to prevent chipping and cracking, a result of having been cast in moulds. To emphasize the sharp perimeters, there is a small gap left at the bottom of the walls so they don't quite meet the floor. And the floors themselves are of large rectangles of York stone, having been laid by masons brought over from England when their French colleagues, not used to this specific stone, had difficulty with the cement fixing.

A long beam of light at the top of the staircase draws customers up. With the staircase's straight, unadorned surface, the steps not quite touching the side walls, the impression is monastic. No wonder then that the monks of Novy Dvur monastery, in the Czech Republic, chose Pawson as the architect of their monastery after they had seen photographs of one of his Calvin Klein boutiques.

Opposite A provocatively posed mannequin lies on a display counter near the entrance of Calvin Klein Paris. **Clockwise from right** The Calvin Klein Home section; a view from the staircase of an internal window; carpets are displayed in custom-designed pull-out frames.

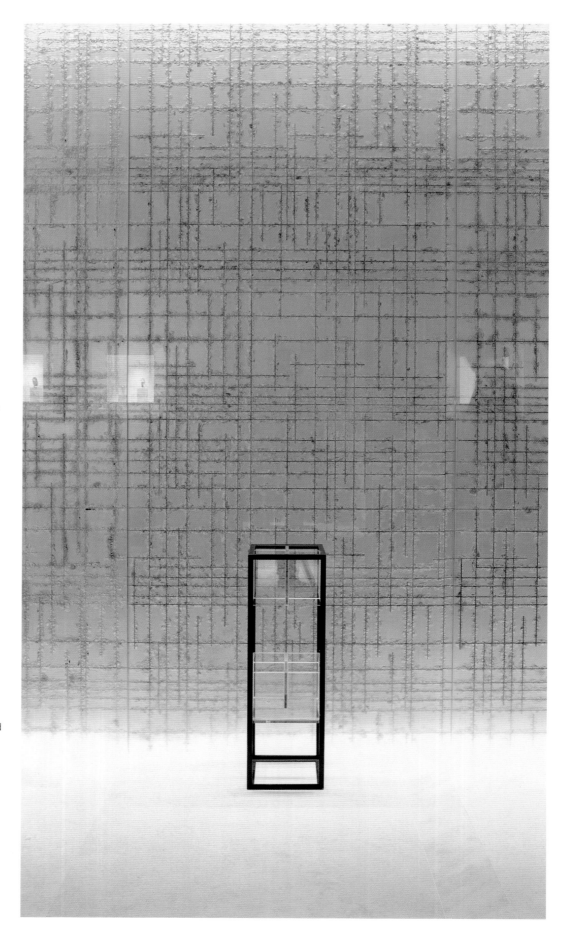

Chanel

rue Cambon
Paris

Peter Marino

This is hallowed ground, where once the venerated Coco Chanel lived and had her salon. Chanel set up her first shop in rue Cambon back in 1910, making the little navy jersey dresses that established her and her style of simplicity. Within a few years she had expanded into the building where today the architect Peter Marino has designed this Chanel boutique.

"I kept running up and down, between Chanel's apartment and the shop," recalls Marino. For just above the boutique are Coco Chanel's living quarters, still preserved as she left them upon her death in 1971 at the age of eighty-eight, and today housing the Chanel archive. Chanel's style came out of what she wore herself; it was very personal. Her apartment is similar, highly individualistic, an extension of her attire in its love of materials, textures and palette. In the grey and amber salons, she heaped cushions of feathers, fur and metallic fabrics upon the sofas, and placed lacquered Chinese red screens. Here she showed the little black dresses, informal cardigan suits and costume jewellery that gained her international recognition. The air was filled with her own perfumes – including Chanel No. 5, the most popular designer fragrance of all time.

Marino has given a modern update on the Chanel apartment, on the Chanel style, in his design for the boutique. He is rather like Karl Lagerfeld, the brilliant fashion designer who took over the House of Chanel in 1983 and transformed it from a faded label into one of the very top fashion collections and sales leaders. Lagerfeld is fond of playing with Chanel's favourite themes: her little dresses and suits, or the nautical chic of Deauville, the once-fashionable French resort on the Pas de Calais where Chanel made such a splash with her early millinery shop.

Peter Marino is an architect with a high and long-standing reputation in the art and fashion world, going back to his time hanging around with Andy Warhol in the 1970s at The Factory in New York. Marino has been designing for Chanel

Opposite Near the entrance of the boutique, a small display stand is placed in front of the glass wall incorporating wide threads of gold leaf, an abstract of a Chanel tweed. Through monochromatic colours and texture, Peter Marino has captured the essence of the late Coco Chanel here in her original *maison de couture*. **Left** The theme of a black and white grid, here separating items in the collection. **Below left** The entrance corridor, with its highly polished Portuguese limestone floors. **Bottom right** A client consultation desk is highlighted by a backlit wall. Handrails are wrapped in black leather.

since 1982, when he did their corporate headquarters offices in New York, going on to create the concept for the Louis Vuitton boutiques and even redesigning Giorgio Armani's private apartments in Milan.

The manner in which Chanel peppered her contemporary-looking apartment with baroque touches fascinates Marino. In homage, at the entrance to the rue Cambon boutique, he created a glass wall incorporating broad 'threads' made of hammered gold leaf, like an exploding Chanel tweed. Gold thread is also entwined into the black carbon-fibre panels that are placed around the boutique.

In fact, the whole boutique is in tones of black and white, another Chanel trademark: white dresses with black trimming; black suits with white trimming; one black earring, one white earring. Floors and floating stairs are of white Portuguese limestone, walls and ceilings lacquered in white diamond dust, vitrines lined in white leather. In the evening wear section, antique silk white organza ribbon is woven into backlit screens.

"In her library", says Marino, speaking of Chanel's apartment, "the books are all behind glass, the cases trimmed in wooden black frames. I trimmed all my display wall units in black leather."

Below Chanel cosmetics on a mirrored display stand of steel frames that were painted black. **Opposite, clockwise from top left** Sunglasses hang on strips of white leather, alternating with strips of black leather featuring white screen-printed logos of the Chanel name; chairs and table designed by Peter Marino; the boutique is a vast sequence of flowing compartments.

Comme des Garçons

rue du Faubourg Saint-Honoré
Paris

**Takao Kawasaki / Rei Kawakubo /
KRD: Shona Kitchen and Abe Rogers**

This boutique is like a great slash of red lipstick on the face of rue du Faubourg Saint-Honoré. Yet it has been applied discreetly, if that seems possible. Down a side alley, with little indication of its location, this Comme des Garçons doesn't flaunt itself to everyone.

"An alien wave entering the space." This was the terse design brief for the Paris Comme des Garçons boutique that Shona Kitchen and Abe Rogers, the partners behind KRD, received on a scribbled bit of paper from fashion designer Rei Kawakubo. And Kawakubo wanted colour. She certainly got want she wanted, especially the colour.

"Red is as strong as black," says Kawakubo, which seems like rather an understatement. But not really so, considering that this was the designer who, having founded Comme des Garçons in 1969, became famous for maintaining a fashion ideology based on black. "There are many blacks, not only one, each black has a shade within it," she once remarked. It was Kawakubo who fuelled the great and long-lasting trend for wearing black during the 1980s and 1990s. Her use of red for this boutique was therefore radical.

Rei Kawakubo has a long tradition of collaborating with well-known architects and designers on her boutiques. Her longest association has been with the architect Takao Kawasaki. At the end of the 1990s she took on the architectural masters of tomorrow's world, Future Systems, who created a metal tunnel for the entrance of her West 22nd Street boutique in New York and also for a corner site on Omotesando in Tokyo, a boutique façade of blue-dotted undulating glass.

In choosing KRD for her Paris boutique, Kawakubo scooped up a pair of young designers who devised a curious concept: part shop, part meditation room – separated yet still a unity. There are two spaces to the boutique, on either side of the courtyard that is down that side alley

off rue du Faubourg Saint-Honoré. The boutique proper lies behind the glazed white steel windows and door; these are obscured by an internal red wall that automatically slides back, allowing you to enter. Ahead is the service counter, the length of the shop, a monolithic red acrylic block with low sections that can be pulled out at varying angles for display and seating. The back wall may be plastered white, and the floor neutral, but the overall effect is created by the red of the opposite wall that wraps up to take in the ceiling. All this in a glossy moulded fibreglass. The display furniture, by Kawakubo, is chromed-steel square tubes with red interiors.

The principal section for presenting the collection is around the corner, in the short length of the L-shaped room. Here garments hang in a white space that is punctuated only by red tubes for displaying shirts and shoes.

The second part of the boutique is across the courtyard, a small room which has been attracting the curiosity seekers: a chamber to decompress from retail shopping. It too is all in blood-red fibreglass, except for the floor. Here there is no merchandise. There is nothing but a series of red cube stools which, when sat upon, suddenly spin and shuffle. It's all a bit magical.

Page 128, top and bottom The front windows and doors at Comme des Garçons Paris are obscured by the back of an interior wall fitting; the service desk with pull-out seating facing the blood-red fibreglass wall and wraparound ceiling.
Page 129 Square steel tubes act as display surfaces and seating. Left Rei Kawakubo broke away from her trademark black with this red interior. Below KRD designed this small room with mechanically moving stools for clients seeking to escape the hustle and bustle of shopping.

Helmut Lang

rue Saint-Honoré
Paris

Gluckman Mayner

The Viennese-born fashion designer Helmut Lang
is building up a repertoire, slowly and consistently,
of clothes and boutiques. Every new collection
that Lang designs appears to be part of a
seamless story. He calls it *séances de travail*,
perhaps best translated as 'a work in progress'.
The changes are subtle, making it usually possible
to mix and wear clothes from several of his
collections without any visual jarring. "I am
progressing, in every collection, towards an
unknown goal which will be the work of my life,"
Lang says with calm assurance.

In 1997, Helmut Lang moved from Paris to
New York, and opened a boutique on Greene
Street in SoHo. His architect was Richard
Gluckman of Gluckman Mayner. This boutique
created quite a stir at the time, and is still much
admired. Gluckman, as a well-known designer
of museums and art galleries including the Andy
Warhol Museum in Pittsburgh, Pennsylvania and
the Georgia O'Keeffe Museum in Santa Fe, New
Mexico, is considered to be a master of display
and space. The New York boutique is an extension
of the gallery aesthetic. No clothing is viewed
from the street or displayed as you enter, there
are only a few works of art placed in the entrance
area – the visitor discovers the collection in a rank
of sleek open wardrobes in the back chamber.

This sense of the enigmatic, of discovery, is
again present in Gluckman's design for the Helmut
Lang boutique in Paris. On a long corner site with
a row of windows on to the street, and within an
historic building that could not be externally
altered, it was more difficult to keep the sense of
the expectant in the design. Gluckman therefore
dramatized the space. Upon entering, the clothes
are not visible. All attention is directed towards
the monolithic staircase. Guarded by two black
sentinel slabs, the concrete stairs run up and
under a massive white structural beam. Both
sides of this black-stained wooden structure are
pierced by openings which serve as the hanging
spaces for the collection on the ground floor.

Opposite A sculpture by Louise Bourgeois hangs in the window, part of a changing display of works by one of Helmut Lang's favourite artists. **Below** The staircase flanked by massive black slabs. The inset handrail features an LED installation by Jenny Holzer. Architect Gluckman Mayer is well known for his work with art galleries, and this boutique exemplifies the present trend of blurring the boundaries between art and fashion.

The first floor is more open than the ground, as it takes over the building next door. Here the principal room is a simple white, with a wall of translucent laminated glass shielding the dressing rooms. Carefully placed in a chequerboard formation are black cubes of vinyl-covered ottomans, for the display of shoes and accessories and, of course, for resting your weary shopping soul.

Sited around the boutique are art installations. There is an interesting series of vintage pieces by the French architect and designer Jean Prouvé (1901–1984), mainly industrial artefacts of lightweight building components: a row of fans mounted on the wall, slatted shutters placed in one of the windows. Helmut Lang has a very fruitful collaboration with two artists, Louise Bourgeois and Jenny Holzer, the three of them having exhibited together at the Vienna Kunsthalle in 1998. The hand-stitched fabric-covered sculptures by Bourgeois, which form part of a rotating series within the boutique, are an obvious link with the fashion designer's world. "For me, sculpture is the body," Bourgeois has said. "My body is my sculpture."

As in all his boutiques, here Lang has mounted an LED installation by Holzer, an artist known for placing her short poetical aphorisms into public spaces. The long LED strip is sliced into the great staircase wall, running alongside the handrail, drawing the visitor forwards to ponder the words as they slide by. Ascending, you catch the phrases 'Je viens . . . Je te vois . . . Je t'explore . . .' then suddenly in reverse, descending as you leave, faster in English 'I flee you . . . I keep your clothes . . .'

Opposite The ground floor display area at Helmut Lang Paris. **Left** Black stools on the upper floor are used for displaying shoes and accessories. **Below** Near the black-and-white sales counter is a wall-mounted fan unit, an industrial artefact designed by the French architect Jean Prouvé.

Jean Paul Gaultier

rue Vivienne
Paris

Philippe Starck

Some marriages are definitely made in heaven.
The association between the fashion designer
Jean Paul Gaultier and the everything designer
Philippe Starck has turned out to be just such
a perfect match. Both are zany Frenchmen,
bouncing with unbridled energy, out to shock
and entertain, divas of design.

Gaultier's style is that of a wayward genius,
his clothes subversive. He is famous for his 'men
in skirts' collection from 1984, and those amazing
conical breasts that Madonna sprouted on her
1990 'Blond Ambition' tour. From street gutter
to high brow, Gaultier snaps it all up. Known
popularly for his Eurotrash style, Gaultier is also
hailed by the fashion cognoscenti as the saviour
of French haute couture.

Starck, too, is a design-dissident celebrity,
splashing his broad product-brush across objects
such as his famously graceful but only semi-
usable lemon-squeezer on stilts. He has created
kettles, watches, even new pasta shapes. As for
interiors and architecture, in the 1970s he got his
start creating Parisian nightclub interiors, moving
on into the 1980s with a series of radically chic
hotels for Ian Schrager. In the 1990s there were
mail-order houses – the kit came with plans,
instructions, a hammer and a flag. And then he
swished into the new millennium with interiors
for the Eurostar terminals in Paris and London.
And much, much more.

Put Gaultier and Starck together and the
result is this cheeky-chic Paris boutique in the
rue Vivienne. The space glitters with crystal
and elegance, with a contrast of hard and soft
surfaces, and a great deal of whimsical wit.

The boutique, which is set in a former
marionette theatre, stands alongside the entrance
to the Galerie Vivienne and is part of this
nineteenth-century shopping arcade, a confection
of cast iron and Neo-classical sculptural relief.
Gaultier had transformed the awkward space in
the 1980s with architects Maurice Marty and
Patrick Le Huérou into a boutique that referenced

Opposite At the end of the main room is a double staircase, with a grotto beneath displaying an oversized Jean Paul Gaultier perfume bottle. The boutique blends wit with sophistication, personal and design characteristics shared by both Gaultier and Starck. **Above** A dressing room with a Stark-designed Louis Ghost chair edged in a silver frame. **Right** The rolling clothing racks and shelves have crystal stems and lights.

Page 138 At the top of the staircase is a multi-coloured screen of mirrors. **Page 139** Display cases are inset with cut-glass panels.

a Pompeian ruin, with mosaic floors that looked partially excavated and mannequins that resembled ancient Roman bronze sculptures.

Starck's re-design is thus transformational, sweeping away the antique for glitz with overtones of Art Deco. Gaultier wanted the sensation of a grotto, in one colour, as if some troll had arrived with a huge sack full of precious objects and spilled the contents all over the place. Starck wanted something simple, favouring his contrasting mixture of raw and shiny.

Thus, in polarity, two visual metaphors dominate the Gaultier boutique: chalk and diamonds. Surfaces are covered in the white chalkiness of Moroccan *tadelakt*, a smooth,

luminous stucco of such durability that Starck used it as a continuous treatment for floor, walls, ceiling, staircase and shelving, hand-smoothed to give gently rounded edges. Integrated into the tall side walls of the principal room are alcoves set with glass display shelves, backed by square padded panels made of taffeta set with a single button in each of their centres.

The effect of diamonds comes from all the reflecting and cut-glass surfaces. Display tables with polished chrome bodies have tops inset with engraved mirror glass. Display cases have drawers fronted by cut mirror. The upright stalks on the rolling clothing racks and shelving units are strings of elongated glass baubles crowned by crystal ball

lamps specially made by the lighting company Flos. Little niches, lined with mirror, hold small display objects. Even Starck's Louis Ghost chairs have been specially adapted to match, with silvered frames and simulated cut-glass backs and seats. But the jewel in the crown is undoubtedly the dazzling screen at the top of the staircase: a patchwork of differently coloured and sized etched mirrors.

And carved out below the double-sweep stairs is a cavern dominated by a giant Jean Paul Gaultier perfume bottle in its distinctive busty corseted shape – an irreverent grotto of Our Lady of Gaultier.

John Galliano

rue Saint Honoré
Paris

**Wilmotte Associés:
Jean-Michel Wilmotte**

The John Galliano boutique comes as quite a shock. This is because it is not a shock. The fashion designer known for his outrageous couture and his own flamboyant personal appearance opened his first boutique in a style that is pure, restrained and only somewhat unusual. How can this be?

Galliano has lost none of his pizzazz. Every fashion season at his shows, models strut down the runway bedecked and swaddled in the most spectacular clothes, painted in exaggerated make-up, shod in fantastic footwear. Galliano's themes have included nuns in bondage, the homeless romanticized, and the London club influences of the late Leigh Bowery and his drag sidekick, Trojan. The clubbing connection is something very special to Galliano, who grew up in 1980s London where, while studying fashion at St Martins College, he punked around with the likes of Bowery.

Galliano seems to have come a long way since then. In 1996 he was made head of one of the most venerable of French *maisons de couture*, the House of Dior. His appointment turned heads in the establishment: such a wild young man! But fashion editors and celebrities loved him and his fashion clothes.

The John Galliano boutique on the corner of rue Saint Honoré and rue Duphot shows Galliano's own label, his second business, so to speak. The clothes speak of a fine balance: the wearable mixed with the bizarre. "I just think every woman

Above The boutique is on a street corner, behind a beautiful historic façade. **Right** At the narrowest point of the interior stands a 5 m tall mirror. **Opposite, top** A kneeling chrome mannequin by Adel Rootstein wears sexy Galliano garments, while behind, floor-to-ceiling video screens show the latest collection. **Opposite, bottom** Near the entrance is the chromed display table.

deserves to be desired. Is that really asking too much?" he remarks in one of his typical statements. So the chrome mannequins in his boutique find themselves lightly draped in signature Galliano outfits based on women's undergarments. Even his men's line has jackets and trousers which fasten with bra hooks and eyes.

So that is the key to the boutique's beautiful style: balance. "Refined is boring and savage can be too obvious," Galliano said around the time he opened this boutique. Helping him to find this balance was the architect Jean-Michel Wilmotte of Wilmotte Associés. Having designed the private apartments in the Elysée Palace for the late President of France François Mitterrand, Wilmotte can certainly claim to be an interiors specialist. He is also an architect with a great deal of experience in display, having created new galleries in the Louvre museum, in Portugal and Korea, and for the king of cognacs, Hennessy.

Wilmotte and his team found their excitable client brimming over with ideas for his new boutique, and once the design process began, Galliano was throwing out ideas and changing his mind at every meeting. *Au fond*, however, was his insistence that the boutique be clean, minimal, and with not much furniture. Materials were therefore restricted: stone, chrome and glass.

And so, the space is simple. Proportionally, it takes the corner wedge of the old building it is in, which is then divided along one side by a balconied first floor. The ground floor is laid with an Italian Paloma stone. The staircase too is stone, and has the only pattern in the boutique, a kaleidoscope of flower-like motifs on the steps, which have been sand-blasted and tinted. 'Flying' over the main space is a glass box, a showcase for display. Also, cutting this central space like high-tech piping are the chromed bars for the clothing racks.

The oddities are discreet. The floor of the dressing room is laid in calf skin, the bathroom walls are covered in hand-stitched embroidery. There are slashes of glass shelving for accessories. And the display tables stand on modern chrome legs but have drawers lined with old-fashioned shagreen, the luxurious scaled skin of the stingray, thus perfectly summing up the balance in style ideas.

Kenzo

rue du Pont-Neuf
Paris

**Jean-Jacques Ory /
DeuxL: Lena Pessoa /
Tiziano Vudafieri / Emmanuelle Duplay**

Unity is not the name of the game at the Kenzo flagship building, which was created by an assortment of architects, designers, styles and ideas. The building houses the Kenzo private offices and showrooms, the Kenzo boutique and two restaurants. Each section, each designer, gently jostles with the other; it's like dipping into a smorgasbord of sensations, all under one roof.

So let's start with the roof, which is a fine work of ribbed cast iron topped by a glass dome. It was built as part of the complete transformation of this building in 1905 by the architect Frantz Jourdain for La Samaritaine, before this department store moved to its present building on rue de la Monnaie. Jordain wrapped the

wedge-shaped structure in a restrained classicism, with vermiculated pilasters and ornate balconies. Gradually over the years, La Samaritaine acquired the adjoining buildings, so that the present Kenzo building now extends into the adjoining buildings with a grand prospect near the River Seine.

The architect for the building's most recent total makeover and restoration was Jean-Jacques Ory, who is known for his sensitive handling of historic French buildings. He created the great central atrium, six storeys in height, triangular in shape following the façade footprint. In the evenings, its plain white surfaces and windows are lit in a glowing green, which gives the exterior an eerie effect. The Kenzo offices take up the greater

Above left A night view of the the Kenzo flagship boutique and offices, which occupy a building that was originally built in the early 1900s for La Samaritaine department store. **Above right, top and bottom** The boutique is in a subdued colour palette. **Opposite, clockwise from top left** The two white *bulles*, or 'bubble' capsules for massage treatments; the golden mosaic interior of one of the *bulles*; the suspended 'UFO' unit for displaying cosmetic and health accessories; a view of LaBulleKenzo, the cosmetics, perfumes and massage area.

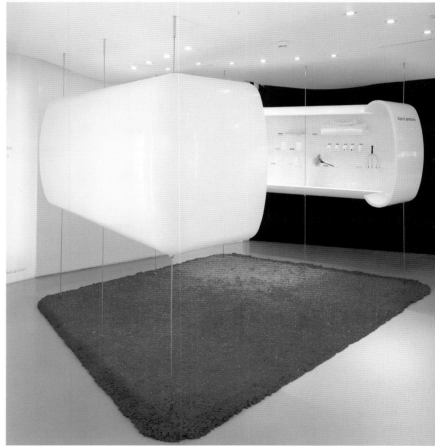

section of the wider part of the building, and busy fashion staff can be seen dashing for the lifts through the full-height glass wall of the atrium.

The Kenzo boutique is in the 'nose' of the building. The architects are Tiziano Vudafieri of Vudafieri Partners from Milan, working with Lena Pessoa's Paris firm of DeuxL. The treatment is subdued, nothing as exciting or cutting edge as the architectural duo's designs for Pucci (see page 146). Each of the four floors carries a different collection – accessories, women, men, casual – with an odd colouring theme of peach and the trademark red of Kenzo.

Superdesign takes over on the other levels. On the fourth level is LaBulleKenzo, dedicated to cosmetics, perfumes and massage. The design intention of this section reads like the entry from the massage menu under 'tactile and climatic variations', which promises 'multiple textures, stimulating shivers and shudders' (1 hour / 100 €). The architect Emmanuelle Duplay has thrown splashes of colours against a white interior for variation, mixed shaggy carpet with smooth plastics for texture, and formed an undulating ceiling for even more movement. As for the shivers and shudders, those can be found in the hanging 'UFO unit' with its contents of 'feather skin strokers' and 'all-terrain cuddlers' (don't ask). And, of course, in the two rounded massage rooms, the massage *bulles*, the bubbles. One is soft inside and out, its exterior hairy, its interior a Kenzo-red, Japanese-like space with a mat on a dark-stained wooden floor that has sunken containers for holding candles. The other is hard, its insides like a golden starburst: the walls, floor and ceiling in a mosaic tile, a revolving glitter ball fracturing the light into diamonds.

When you emerge, as the massage menu tells us, from your experience in an 'exit state' of either 'sensory drowsiness, lingering smile' or 'exhilarated and carried away', the Kenzo building gives you a choice of rather similar places to replenish your body. Down in the lower level is the quiet Japanese restaurant, Lô Sushi, and at the very top is the more gregarious Kong restaurant-bar, both by well-known French designers.

Lô Sushi is by Andrée Putman. The food is served in the *kaiten-zushi* method, on circulating conveyor belts that meander through an off-white interior. Actually, the restaurant looks like a small financial trading floor, with banks of computer screens, one per high-stool customer. The idea is that you can do your e-mails while slurping your miso soup. Or, more daringly, e-mail a fellow chopstick twiddler.

But the best treat is under that curved iron and glass roof, at the Kong restaurant. Not only are the views wonderful and the food good, but Philippe Starck's design gives you a good

chuckle. His Louis XV-style Louis Ghost chairs are of transparent polycarbonate, and on the entire two floors, the backs of the chairs and the clear bands at the back of the booths are peppered with *trompe-l'œil* images of punky Japanese girls' heads.

Below, clockwise from top Kenzo Paris's Lô Sushi restaurant, with its banks of computer screens; a Philippe Starck chair in the Kong restaurant; Japanese dining designed by Andrée Putman. **Opposite** The spectacular glass-panelled roof of the Starck-designed Kong restaurant.

Left The boutique façade. **Below** Acrylic shelves are held in place by steel cables. **Opposite** The rounded edges of the counters and display units are echoed in the inset ceiling panels above. The delicate display system and coloured lighting scheme complement the vibrant textiles in the Pucci range.

Pucci

avenue Montaigne
Paris

DeuxL: Lena Pessoa / Tiziano Vudafieri

Psychedelic patterns. Vibrant colours. Feathery fabrics. The clothing range of the house of Pucci is among the most intensely vivacious of all fashion lines. It takes a careful stylist to show such a collection to its best, avoiding a riotous collision of different styles. So the designer of this Paris boutique, Lena Pessoa, chose a quiet approach. "Serenity was our goal," she said, "not dramatic effects."

This was Pessoa's eighth fashion boutique for the LVMH empire, which acquired the house of Pucci in 2000; Pucci's daughter Laudomia still runs the firm from the family's ancient palazzo in the shadow of Florence's Duomo. Pessoa's Paris-based firm, DeuxL, teamed up with architect Tiziano Vudafieri of Vudafieri Partners for this little boutique on a grand street. Inheriting a 150 m² (1600 sq ft) former shoe shop, the pair purified the interior by removing upright structures, making an expansive, unbroken space. Then they set about creating a translucent backdrop, putting the collection, not their own work, on show.

Pessoa and Vudafieri have created a remarkable space, subtle, glowing from within. The furniture is virtually all made in clear or sanded acrylic. The edges are rounded; drawers are slipped open with recessed slots, not protruding knobs, and are beautifully lined within. Counters are coolly smooth, sprayed with automotive paint.

The minimizing extends to the acrylic poles from which the thin clothing rails are suspended. Hanging off steel cables, the clear acrylic shelves displaying the Pucci accessories are uplit so that they radiate in shades of a Pucci scarf – pink, blue and white.

The overall lighting, which keeps the boutique washed in tranquility, is the design of consultant Walter Amort of Studio Emotional Lighting. He lined the walls with a sheer, fireproofed fabric in a satin finish, downlit from fluorescent recessed lighting in the ceiling.

Pessoa chooses varying colours for the overall tone of each of the Pucci boutiques she

designs. For the Paris shop, it is a soft aqua. "I brought in the sea," she remarks. And the sea is a very appropriate analogy, for it was on the isle of Capri, in the warm Mediterranean waters, that Emilio Pucci, Marquese di Barsento, opened one of his first boutiques, in 1949, selling clothes of his own design. His Capri pants were a sensation. During the 1950s, Pucci gained a reputation for brightly coloured and boldly patterned prints, particularly in lightweight silks, polyester and nylon. And so he continued, opening boutiques in the most fashionable of the jet-setting resorts. By the 1960s, he had branched into shoes, purses, luggage, bathing suits, nightgowns and lingerie. The six ranges of hostess uniforms that he created for Braniff Airways between 1965 and 1974, including the famous plastic bubble headdress, helped to reconfigure fashion to a space age look.

A sense of the historical tradition of Emilio Pucci, who died in 1992, and his importance to modern couture and *prêt-à-porter*, pervades the Paris boutique. Foremost, of course, is Pucci's fashion line, which continues today with Christian Lacroix designing in the flamboyant spirit of the founder. And then there are the stars who wear Pucci, past and present, whose portraits line the boutique walls: Madonna, Sophia Loren and Marilyn Monroe, whose unmistakable figure lounges on a bed, wearing Pucci shirt and trousers.

The architect Lena Pessoa chose a gentle aqua for the overall colour scheme at Pucci Paris, as a cool background for the hot colours of the collection.

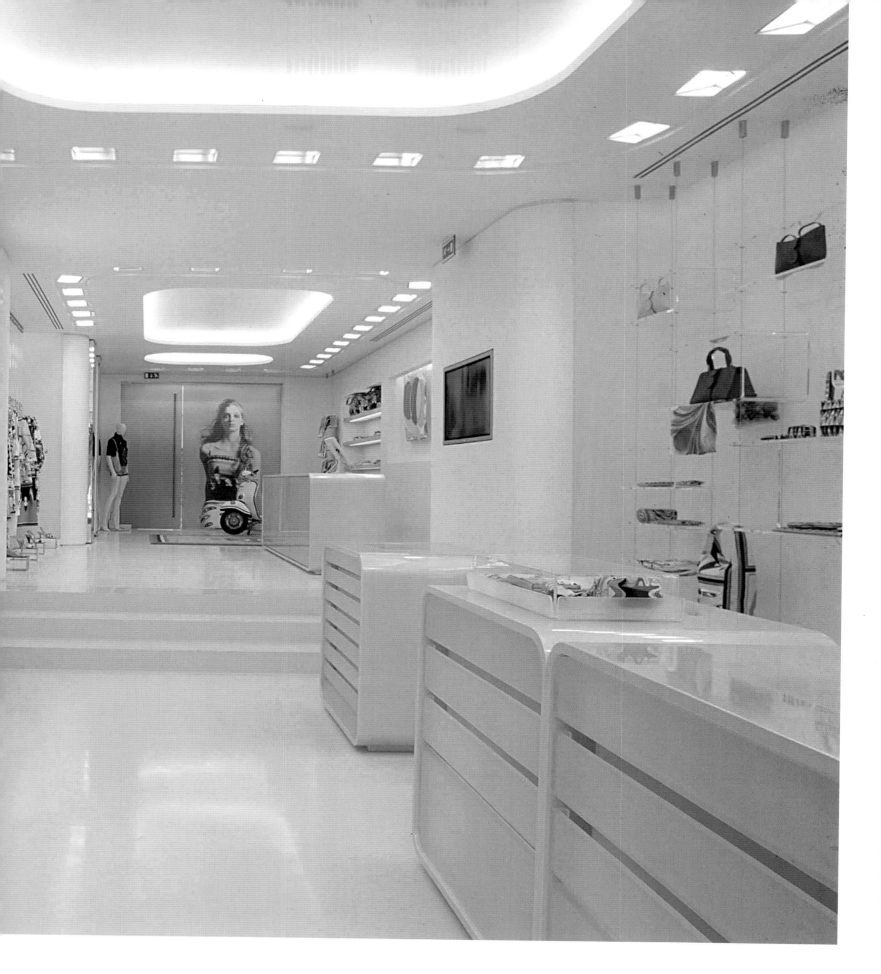

TOKYO

Celux
Tim Power with Eric Carlson and David McNulty

Christian Lacroix
CAPS: Christophe Carpente

Dior
SANAA/Architecture & Associés

Hussein Chalayan
Block Architecture

Louis Vuitton
Jun Aoki/Louis Vuitton Département d'Architecture

Maison Hermès
Renzo Piano Building Workshop/Rena Dumas Architecture Intérieure

Prada Epicenter
Herzog & de Meuron

Y's
Arad Associates: Ron Arad and Asa Bruno

Celux

Omotesando
Tokyo

**Tim Power with Eric Carlson
and David McNulty**

To label Celux a private members' club makes it sound stuffy. There are certainly no overstuffed leather chairs filled with snoozing gentlemen here. More apt would be to call it a private members' boutique.

Perched atop the Louis Vuitton Omotesando boutique (see page 170), Celux is where Nu-Lux meets fashion: the latest concept to sprout from the boutique scene, aimed at the most exclusive end of the luxury market. Membership is not only for those who can afford its steep fee, but also for cool fashionistas after the latest and hard-to-get fashion pieces. As the brainchild of the Louis Vuitton Japan group, the emphasis on the brands available obviously concentrates on their holdings: Louis Vuitton, Dior, Kenzo. Mixed in among them are hot emerging designers from around the world. Celux is a place to come and shop, relax over a drink, flip through a style magazine, meet others with your interest in fashion, and party. It is reported that sixty per cent of members are men.

The American-born architect Tim Power, who is now based in Milan, has created a special place with his beautiful design. "I wanted to express a different expectation of what is luxury," he comments. Following the dichotomy in today's fashion world, especially strong in Japan where haute couture often entwines with street culture, Power mixed "high with low, luxury materials with inexpensive materials, salon with street".

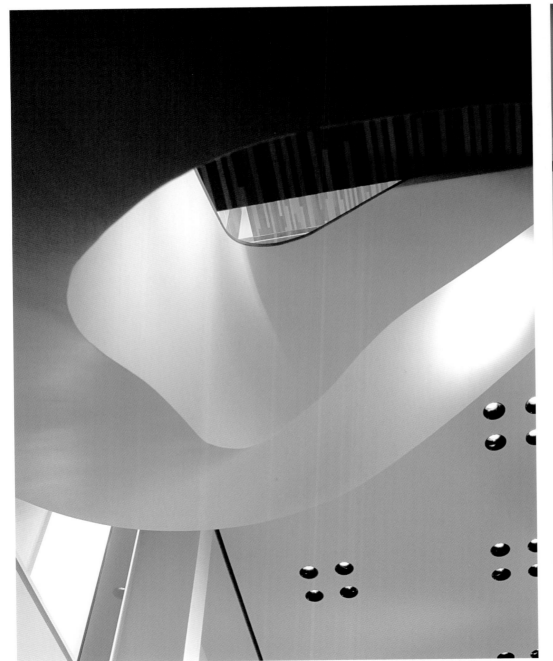

Left The dramatic curves of the underside of the staircase. **Above** A washroom. **Opposite** The lower level of this private members' boutique is mainly for displaying collections. The walnut finish is a band which begins as a floor, rises up the end wall and then wraps round the ceiling of the upper level.

Celux is on two floors, both double height. Members enter via a private lift to the uppermost storey and into the almost Art Deco-style lobby, with its curved linoleum-clad walls and stainless steel banding. Beyond is the lounge. Here the expanse of windows is framed within frames, creating shelving for displaying objects with a backdrop of views across Tokyo, seen through the fine mesh that screens the Jun Aoki-designed building. The opposite interior wall has more object display below and inexpensive acoustic tiling above, inset with pinpoint lighting. This wall can be transformed into a shelving system for clothing when the space is required. At one end is the bar, and a little stainless steel balcony for taking drinks.

Thanks to the furnishings and decorative accessories by Eric Carlson and David McNulty, the interior has a retro-chic feeling reminiscent of a collaboration between the decorator Piero Fornasetti and the industrial designer Gio Ponti. Vintage 1950s Eames pieces mix with new Pucci-print chairs and settees; there are rows of glass and ceramic pots and vases, framed pictures and *objets trouvés*. Everything is for sale.

Not wishing to lose precious floor space, Power designed a steep sweep to the staircase leading to the sales boutique floor below. The staircase is a masterly piece of craftsmanship fabricated in northern Japan, with every steel step a different size, and then covered in soft white felt. The parabolic curve of the staircase spins around the colourful Venini glass bobbles of the 1950s chandelier.

The staircase is not the only link between the two floors. A wide strip of black walnut wraps both spaces together, a powerfully rich feature. It begins at the entrance wall, floats over the top storey, and then descends in the staircase cut, down the end wall, transforming into the floor of the showroom.

Tempted to join this fashion boutique in the sky? Celux membership costs about ¥200,000, approximately US$1800, plus substantial annual dues. And you have to go through the interview, or in Japanese, *o-miai* – the traditional matchmaking ceremony.

Opposite The entrance lobby of Celux Omotesando, with its stainless steel banding. **Below left** The small balcony for taking drinks. **Below** The upper level, where Pucci fabric covers the furniture, is for relaxing.

Christian Lacroix

Daikanyama
Tokyo

CAPS: Christophe Carpente

"Patchwork et métissages unique liberté couleur individualité et calligraphie, rite profondeur rare personalité, non pas diktat mais créativité, le sud", reads the big, bold, handwritten message by the French designer Christian Lacroix across the three-storey glass façade of his Tokyo boutique. Loosely translated: "Patchwork and melting pot, unique freedom colour individuality and calligraphy, formal depth rare personality, not dogma but creativity, the South".

It's a powerfully poetic and quirky statement of values, reinforcing those of the designer who is renowned in his field for keeping his own liberty and individuality in the skittish and corporate-driven world of fashion. Although his fashion house is part of the LVMH empire, Lacroix is celebrated for not following trends, but rather for sustaining a rich and luscious style, one of the few designers to carry on the legacy of French haute couture. With a strong background in art history (a higher degree from his native *sud* – as he makes passing reference to in his message), and as a designer of costumes for opera and ballet, Lacroix is an authority on, and interpreter of, past styles from a variety of worldwide regions.

Cross-culturalism and colour influences are trademarks of Lacroix's ethos. And these are the two principal impressions of this boutique. As a starting example, we need only look at that billboard-size calligraphy: in terms of cross-cultural

Above The enlarged handwritten poem by Christian Lacroix on the glass façade of the boutique, although written in French, makes reference to the art of Japanese calligraphy. **Right and opposite** The plexiglas furniture is edged in brushed stainless steel.

interpretation, admittedly it is written in French and therefore not understood by most of the passing Japanese, but they no doubt recognize the artistic reference to their own treasured tradition in calligraphy. And the lettering may be white, but because it is on holographic film, the wall shimmers in rainbow slices, splattering the interior with colour.

The architect, Christophe Carpente of Zürich-based CAPS (Corporate Architecture and Project Management Services), was responsible for interpreting Lacroix's design and retail concepts. "He was in search of clear lines," remarks Carpente of his client, "and of baroque minimalism." Now, if ever there was a contradiction in stylistic terms, 'baroque minimalism' – in other words, excessive little – must be it.

Thus Carpente chose to create display furniture that was transparent but colourful, an interior of chromatic layering, like one of Lacroix's evening dresses layered in luxuriant materials and enveloped in waves of colour. The fittings are perspex, a spectrum of red, orange, yellow, green, blue, violet – "Ali Baba colours," muses the architect. Some of the edges, and all of the round-cornered interior shelves, are encased in brushed stainless steel, so that the reflections do not fall on the merchandise. These display units can be moved about the boutique; they are nomadic, part of the theme of cross-culturalism. In the same vein, the dressing rooms are tents, opulently lined with pink silk.

All this colour is shown against a neutral background of walls and ceiling. A few classic chairs by Pierre Paulin, sinuous and colourful, break the angularity of the display furniture. Changing presentations by artists working in oils, photography and video transform the boutique into a gallery, making Lacroix's garments and accessories become part of an exhibition.

Opposite, top and bottom, and left The rainbow of coloured perspex of the display units creates a kaleidoscope effect and keeps the space light and uncrowded. **Above** In the corner is the changing room, resembling a nomadic tent lined with pink silk.

Dior

Omotesando
Tokyo

SANAA/Architecture & Associés

The Dior boutique in Tokyo Omotesando is a ballgown trimmed with tulle ribbons by fashion designer John Galliano. Or, at least, it is an architectural metaphor of such by the architects Kazuyo Sejima and Ryue Nishizawa, known as SANAA. Asked by representatives at Dior for a new building which was feminine, elegant and intimate, Sejima and Nishizawa chose a ballgown from John Galliano's debut collection for Dior in 1997 as their design source.

Dior is a classic fashion house. Classic, but not traditional. Since the death of the great couturier Christian Dior in 1957, the reins of design have passed from one famous name to the next: Yves Saint Laurent, Marc Bohan, Gianfranco Ferré, and now Hedi Slimane in Dior Homme and, since 1996, the wild young John Galliano, who especially has done so much to lift and change Dior into an extremely desirable label.

So today the look of Dior is a bit of yesterday, a bit of tomorrow. Like this Tokyo Dior boutique. From the exterior, SANAA's seven-storey building is an extremely contemporary structure, a smooth glass tower rippling with the texture and flounce of dress material, a result of the glass having been pressed with an acrylic thermoformed lining. It is almost is if the building had been neatly wrapped from within by the artist Christo.

Inside, the design is classic with a twist, the creation of Architecture & Associés who are

Left The whole of the glass façade of the Dior boutique is internally coated with an acrylic thermoformed lining to give the effect of dress material. **Opposite** The interior is a series of classic rooms, like stage sets, evoking the famous salons of the venerable Dior boutique in Paris.

Opposite The staircase at Dior Omotesando is a mixture of old and new styles, with wood-panelled walls, mirrored understairs and glass showcases. **Top right** Strips of plasma screens act as a room divider in the women's section. **Bottom right** A whirlpool ceiling light of polished stainless-steel rings dominates the perfume and cosmetics area.

responsible for many Dior interiors. The two principal architects of the firm, Pierre Beucier and Jean-Christophe Poggioli, evoke the famous Dior boutique on the avenue Montaigne in Paris, which is well known for its series of rooms. There, of course, the rooms are actual, with structural walls, while within the Tokyo tower, the rooms are freestanding, like stage sets.

Partitions are reminiscent of old panelling, yet may be suddenly sliced off through their sections, with perfectly cut stainless steel mirrors along their edges even taking up the outline of the cornice. Everything seems to sparkle with light. The floors are of stone, highly glossed and reflective. Backlit panels display accessories. Table cases are sheathed in mirror, sometimes with etched patterning. The handrails and under-surface of the stairs are mirrored. In the perfume and cosmetics section, the room is dominated by a whirlpool ceiling light fixture of polished stainless steel rings. Cosmetics are set into shelving that reflects the product towards infinity. The facial room is a hoop of so many floor-to-ceiling segmental mirrors that clients must feel like they are in a fun fair of fashion.

And a high-tech dose has been injected into the atmosphere. Images are projected on to walls, plasma screens show the latest collections. Strips of plasma screens make a crazy room divider, displaying slit-images of fashion shows. In the dressing rooms there are no mirrors; instead the Belgian artist Carsten Höller, known for his interactive installations, has created boxes on which customers find themselves projected at three-second intervals.

In the men's section at lower level, Hedi Slimane, fashion designer for Dior Homme, has worked the room in strips of light and dark achieved through the intensity of mirrored and lacquered surfaces: white acrylic shelving, dark stone floor, intensely lit white ceiling. And, playfully, when customers seat themselves on the benched surfaces, they are showered with electronic music and crimson lighting.

Which all goes to show that the *grande dame* of Dior still knows how to wear her ballgown with dazzling style.

Opposite and below Hedi Slimane, the chief designer for Dior Homme, designed the black-and-white theme of the men's section at Dior Omotesando. The speakers in the sides of the mirrored units come to life and lights flash when unsuspecting clients sit on the benched surfaces.

Hussein Chalayan

Daikanyama
Tokyo

Block Architecture

Hussein Chalayan, the young British fashion designer, opened his first boutique in Tokyo. The Japanese, with their love of the quirky and quixotic, adore his clothes. You might remember seeing Chalayan present his collections, so innovative that they made the nightly news reports: models swathed in his versions of black Islamic dress complete with the veiled chador. Or his performance show with a living room where the models stepped into the wooden chairs and coffee tables that morphed into dresses.

It's all part of Chalayan's obsession with cultural displacement and transformation, rooted in his own background as a Turkish Cypriot transplanted on British soil. No wonder, then,

that he hit it off so well with Graeme Williamson and Zoë Smith of Block Architecture, who describe their approach to the design of his new shop as "taking cultural references that people understand, then twisting and reappraising them in a new way."

Together, fashion designer and architects have created a little bit of somewhere – somewhere else. In the bustling district of Daikanyama you will find a lazy summer's day on a Mediterranean isle, populated by many beautiful frocks. The Hussein Chalayan boutique shimmers with Cypriot references in a Japanese context.

And much more, for Chalayan and Block have other feathers in their designers' caps. Especially the sensations of mobility and travel … because

営業時間
11:00 ～ 20:00

OPENING HOURS
11:00 ～ 20:00

to be displaced, you must make the journey. The direction-finders for the boutique are the name-signs in the windows, 'Hussein Chalayan' in English and in Japanese, modelled on the bright yellow lightboxes that guide us through airports. Continuing the rite of passage, the visitor steps into the shop alongside the double-height 'aeroplane wall', a play on another of the fashion designer's travel obsessions, aeroplane parts. The wall is like looking out of the plane window on to the wing, an assemblage of angled metal sheets riveted together. But on this wing-wall, the piston arms act as brackets for the shelving flaps.

And so we have arrived. The tiled entrance ramp has been a trip up the red, white and black pattern of a backgammon board, a favourite gaming pastime in Cyprus. Spread before us is an olive grove, live trees springing from beneath the herringbone parquet flooring. Washing lines are strung with clothes. A few rough rope chairs handmade in Cyprus. Up the stairs to a small 'outdoor' cinema showing Chalayan's films.

Now it's time to send greetings home ... pick an 'airmail T-shirt' out of the selection on the back wall, Chalayan-designed, packaged and ready to post. And add your own message: "Dear Friends, wish you could be here."

Page 166 In a nod to Hussein Chalayan's fascination with the notion of travel and displacement, yellow airport-style signage marks the entrance to his Daikanyama boutique.
Page 167 The entrance, with its striped flooring like a backgammon board, lies below the 'airplane wall' of fold-down metal wing flaps that are used as display shelving.

Opposite and right The Hussein Chalayan collection is displayed on rope tied between metal poles, like washing hanging out to dry, while little trees grow through the floor — all in evocation of the sunny island culture of Chalayan's Turkish Cypriot background.

Louis Vuitton

Omotesando
Tokyo

Jun Aoki / Louis Vuitton Département d'Architecture

In the museum display of Louis Vuitton vintage products in this Tokyo store is a selection of unique historical trunks: there is one made in 1888 for the French explorer Count Pierre Savorgnan de Brazza that turns into a bed; another from 1937 for a Cuban diplomat and film-maker that transforms into a desk incorporating a typewriter, film projector and wireless radio; and, designed in 1939 for King Farouk of Egypt, a trunk that metamorphoses into an office.

Trunk upon trunk upon trunk – this is an image highlighted by the architect Jun Aoki who, in creating the external appearance of this nine-storey building, has stacked together various box-shaped spaces. To distinguish each of these 'trunks', as Aoki actually refers to them, is a wrapping in a different 'lining': the ground floor, for example, is in Damier check, one of the classic Louis Vuitton patterns. Astonishingly, the linings are all woven in metal mesh. Their texture is reinforced behind by polished panels of stainless steel, some of which are treated in coloured surfaces of silvery copper and golden pink.

The meshing – an adaptation of a material originally used to make conveyor belts in factories that process almonds dipped in chocolate – is a favourite motif within Louis Vuitton boutiques. As is the theme of the trunk. The interior architects from the Louis Vuitton Département d'Architecture, under the principals Eric Carlson and David McNulty, are well versed in designing for retail success and know how to reinforce the brand look, based on a concept by the architect Peter Marino that draws the customer further and further into the shop. The entrance space is voluminous, double height and with walls cut with large openings in those ubiquitous trunk-shaped squares and rectangles. It is these openings that are hung with meshing. Once in the memory, even the display tables and counters start to take on the outline of these large travelling containers. Many of the walls are subtly plastered

Below and opposite By layering elongated boxed forms one upon another to create the exterior silhouette of the boutique, the architect Jun Aoki honours the travelling trunks that first made Louis Vuitton famous. These 'trunks' are covered in differing patterns of woven wire mesh.

in alternating matt and glossy squares, textured and stripped, again an adaptation of the Damier check: wall as handbag.

The Japanese are mad about Louis Vuitton luxury commodities. There is something neatly conservative and old-European about LV and, under the fashion design eye of Marc Jacobs, the clothing is neatly styled. There are more than three hundred Louis Vuitton boutiques in fifty countries, but nearly a sixth are in Japan. And the Omotesando store is the company's premier flagship in the country.

The boutique takes up the first five levels. On the upper floors, true exclusivity reigns in the members-only club, Celux (see page 152). Aoki created the intervening space for product launches and parties with cubed wall of wenge, walnut and moabi woods. Suspended in one section is a glass enclosure which, to the great amusement of onlookers, slowly descends to become a changing room. Maintaining the theme of 'lining', the translucent cage is shrouded with white linen. The fashion-meets-architecture imagery never ends.

Below The spacious interior of Louis Vuitton Omotesando has walls with large cut-out sections that have then been glazed. **Opposite** In the VIP quarters, a suspended dressing room can be lowered at the touch of a switch.

The Louis Vuitton Omotesando boutique has five levels of luxury retailing, linked by a central staircase. Walls are textured in alternating shiny and matt squares of wall plaster in a pattern similar to a Louis Vuitton City bag.

Maison Hermès

Ginza
Tokyo

Renzo Piano Building Workshop/
Rena Dumas Architecture Intérieure

The special glass blocks which form the skin of the Maison Hermès boutique in Tokyo are rumoured to be the exact size of one of Hermès's famous silk scarves when folded. "It's a myth," responds Rena Dumas, the interior architect of the structure, "but such a pleasing one you have to believe it."

Actually, the real myth-maker in the case of Hermès is the architect Renzo Piano, responsible for such renowned buildings as the Centre Georges Pompidou in Paris (created back in the mid-1970s with Richard Rogers) and his more recent mammoth Kansai International Airport near Osaka. Piano is known for innovative engineering feats, and the Hermès building certainly extends his status.

Hermès is a much venerated French fashion label. Founded in the 1840s by Thierry Hermès, a maker of harnesses and saddles to European royalty, the company gently altered direction in the early twentieth century when horse-power gave way to the motorcar and new forms of travel. Trunks and luggage, beautifully crafted, became the mainstay. By the 1960s, the likes of Grace Kelly and Jackie Onassis were photographed wearing Hermès scarves (launched in 1937) and holding Hermès bags, making the Kelly bag and the Jackie-O bag must-have accessories. Today, the Maison Hermès has diversified into fashion clothing (given a real boost by the designer Martin Margiela for six years, until 2003), perfumes, even furniture. But it is the bespoke and limited-edition bags that are the top-sellers. When this Hermès boutique opened in the Ginza district of Tokyo, people queued overnight to snatch up Kelly bags at ¥500,000 (approximately US$5000) … and they sold out so fast that many shoppers came away disappointed.

Hermès is still family run, by Jean-Louis Dumas. Rena Dumas is his wife, who has styled the interiors of the Hermès boutiques for more than twenty years. The initial concept for the Japan boutique emerged when she and Renzo

Opposite The glass-block grid of the twelve-storey façade of the Maison Hermès Ginza glows at night. Renzo Piano and Rena Dumas found the inspiration for using glass blocks when they visited the famous Maison de Verre in Paris, designed by Pierre Chareau in the 1920s. **Below** The interior is furnished in classic Maison Hermès style, with all the fittings pulled away from the glass-block walls.

Piano visited La Maison de Verre in Paris, the 'house of glass' by Pierre Chareau. It was the famous little façade of glass blocks from that gem of 1920s Modernism that Piano translated to Tokyo.

In fact, Piano inflated his glass-block façade to twelve storeys, and wrapped it around the corner of a prominent Ginza intersection, a slim crystal brother rising next to the landmark 1960s Sony Building. And whereas the old Parisian glass blocks were quite small, Piano made his, if not quite folded scarf size, a substantial 428 mm (about 17 in.) square. Then came the engineering feat. The blocks, all 13,000 of them, are not load-bearing, but suspended off the concrete and steel tower which lies to the side. Thus the blocks didn't need any grout between them, as they are encased in latticed steel units. In addition, the whole is engineered to withstand earthquakes. With the only clear glass being the display windows around the entrance, the translucent blocks make the whole of the Hermès building glow from within when lit at night.

The boutique interior consists of the traditionally tasteful wood display tables and wall units found throughout the Hermès empire. Dumas, however, has pulled the furniture away from the glass walls, adding a greater three-dimensional feel to the space. On the fifth floor is a small museum, devoted to historical pieces from the Hermès collection, sitting in display cases that have plinths of small glass blocks. On the floors above are an exhibition space, workshops for Hermès craftsmen and a roof garden.

Over the recessed forecourt and suspended almost the height of the building is a mobile sculpture by artist Susuma Shingo. And, way at the top, overlooking the main thoroughfare, is an equestrian sculpture, a colourful horseman bearing a pair of flag standards of actual Hermès scarves.

Opposite, left Fine glass goblets sit upon the glass shelves at Maison Hermès Ginza, backed by a wall of glass blocks. **Opposite, right** The reflecting pool in the private quarters. **Left** An etched-glass drawing reminding visitors that Maison Hermès began as a saddlers. **Below** In the museum, historic Hermès pieces are displayed in cases set on glass blocks.

Prada Epicenter

Aoyama

Tokyo

Herzog & de Meuron

Could this be the most beautiful of all boutiques? The most successful? The most influential? Whatever the judgement, there is no doubt that the Aoyama Prada is a major work of new architecture, a building foretelling things to come.

This is the second of the great Prada Epicenters, following on from Rem Koolhaas's design for New York. For their biggest venture – in fact, reputedly Italy's biggest retail investment in Japan since the Second World War – Miuccia Prada and her husband Patrizio Bertelli, chief executive of Prada, turned to Jacques Herzog and Pierre de Meuron. In the topsy-turvy architectural muddle and confusion that is Tokyo, these Swiss architects have bestowed upon the city a landmark building and, a rarity for Japan, a small public space. Herzog & de Meuron placed their six-and-a-bit-storey Prada building on the edge of the site, giving room for a green space of neatly textured moss surfaces set in flagstones. "Ultimately," explains Herzog, "the building was treated like a plant, placed where conditions are best for it to grow into what we wanted it to become."

The boutique is an expensive, odd-shaped little parcel tied with string – just the thing that the Japanese, with their love of wrapping, can appreciate. Actually, the exterior is a lattice 'binding' of steel diamonds each inset with glass: flat, convex and concave. None of the sides of the

Left A twilight view of the prismatic tower of Prada Aoyama. This is the New Boutique as outstanding architecture. With Herzog & de Meuron's innovative design, Prada has once again advanced the image of the luxury fashion world. **Above** The internal staircase follows the line of the external steel web. **Opposite, top** The garden plaza with the greenery of moss carpets. **Opposite, bottom** The distorting optics of the convex and concave glass modules.

building is the same size, width or height; the roof is just an extension of the façades. When the boutique is viewed from the outside, the floor levels are clearly seen, as are the staircases and three tunnels which cross at different planes from one side to another. And, of course, the merchandise and clientele are on full display, quirkily distorted by the bubbling glass.

On the inside, the steel web is lacquered in satin white. And with the expanse of carpeting, fittings and furniture also in white and cream, the effect is pure and light. Unique are the low display tables, made of fibreglass of a gelatinous appearance, illuminated from within, with a series of differently sized inset drops and shelves.

Fittings at Prada Epicenter Aoyama are streamlined and kept low around the perimeter, to allow customers good views out of the windows and to the back of the boutique. The recesses in the display tables are loosely based on the punch-out packaging used for pills and tablets.

Privacy and intimate space for relaxing and trying on clothes are contained within the three flying corridors, which also structurally assist in tying the building together. Shaped in the same rhomboid section as the exterior windows, these are 'architectural caverns' set in the space age. Dressing rooms have optically controlled glass doors, similar to the famous ones in Prada Epicenter New York, changing from clear to opaque at the touch of a button (see page 108). In the flying corridors, leaning back into the soft banquettes, you will find the best place for 'snorkelling'. Pull over the long flexible arm of a 'snorkel', the IT monitor, and watch, listen and be seduced by information on the Prada collection.

And the influence of this Prada? At the same time as Herzog & de Meuron were working on Prada Tokyo, they were beginning their designs for the 2008 Beijing Olympic Stadium. "The Prada boutique was a laboratory," Herzog says broadly. "It fed us ideas for our stadium."

Opposite Video screens on flexible arms, nicknamed 'snorkels', snake down from the ceiling. **Below** One of the three tubular corridors that run across the building's width, containing rest areas, 'snorkels' and changing rooms.

Y's

Roppongi Hills
Tokyo

Arad Associates:
Ron Arad and Asa Bruno

"I like my clothing to be in a spirit close to Zen. Let's be quiet," comments Yohji Yamamoto in a hushed tone, sounding like a Zen master. This fashion designer, who opened his first boutique in Paris in 1981, has maintained his tranquil strength through using a restricted colour palette, particularly black, or black and white, a concept developed alongside his close friend Rei Kawakubo of Comme des Garçons. And, also typical of the great Japanese fashion designers – like Kawakubo and Issey Miyake – Yamamoto is skilled in the gentle art of tailoring, using abstracted forms rather than brash and strident gestures.

It was this quiet approach that Yamamoto also adopted with the architects for his boutique in Roppongi Hills, Tokyo, giving Arad Associates the freedom of architectural design without imposing his fashion will upon them. All he asked was that the architects come up with a new way of displaying his collection. Which they did – in a most intriguing and fantastic way.

Ron Arad is an architect who is as well known for his furniture and lighting designs as he is for his household items for Alessi. There is always a quirky *joie de vivre* about his work. Right from the onset in his early notable designs from the 1980s, metal tube construction played a major role, as in his Rover Chair, a car seat with bent scaffolding poles as legs and arms. In Y's boutique, Arad has had a field day with tubular

Opposite and right Three giant towers of spinning tubular bars act as clothing rails for Yamamoto's collection, putting the clothes in motion as if they were being worn by ghostly bodies. The colour palette of the boutique is restricted, except for the flamboyant shock of the furniture, reception desk and the logo on the entrance doors.

bars, making them fan out and swirl in the sculptural forms of the display units that command the interior space.

There are four of these hula-hoop champions. Three of them embrace the concrete structural columns of the new thirty-storey residential tower above. Each unit is composed of a layering of thirty-four aluminium hoops of oval shape, which are the clothing rails. Aluminium shelves can be inserted in the openings for table display. Staff can arrange the hoops as they wish, in cascading tiers or randomly.

And then, the units spin, smoothly and quietly. Each sits upon a circular motorized turntable that speeds up at night, making the boutique pulsate like a club-goer's heart on Ecstasy.

Wishing to offset the subdued shades of Yamamoto's style, Arad Associates introduced bursts of coloured intensity into the boutique. As visitors enter, they are confronted with the looping Y logo, in bright colours, laminated into the revolving glass doors. The reception desk is an intense red. A long L-shape form, measuring 8 m by 6 m (26 x 20 ft), it too has that layered look of the hanging units, being composed of twenty-two slabs of hollow mild steel sections set slightly displaced from one another. And then there are the bright lime-green chairs and ottomans, designed by Arad, manufactured by Bonaldo and named Ron-Aldodown.

The boutique windows have an undulating movement, the glass a row of semicircular vertical tubes set into round bases that hold mannequins or display objects. The changing rooms also take on the theme of the vertical curve, with tall, S-shaped doors, or 'gills' as the architects refer to them, that do not close. The customer steps between these vents, which overlap for privacy and, as an added caution against intrusion, the edge has an LED strip that changes from green to red when someone enters.

The spinning tubular hoops of the three towers are used as clothing rails; shelves for displaying accessories can be added or removed.

ACKNOWLEDGEMENTS

The suggestion for writing this book came from Mark Fletcher, my commissioning editor, whom I would like to thank for his continuing support.

To the fashion designers, architects and designers, all of whom patiently answered my questions and gave me their views on the New Boutique, I give my grateful thanks.

On the front line, I met the friendly staff of many luxury boutiques around the world, all of whom, without exception, extended kindness and helpfulness.

At Merrell Publishers, I would like to thank heartily editorial director Julian Honer for acting as a guiding light; Marion Moisy, project manager, for her sympathetic expertise; Nicola Bailey, design manager, for helping to shape the book; and Hugh Merrell, Sam Wythe, Matt Packer and Paul Shinn for their collaboration.

To Maggi Smith, to whom I am most appreciative for the beautiful design of this book.

And to my dear friends who contributed by their comments, put me up and put up with me when I was researching and writing this book: in Amsterdam, Dirk van den Heuval; in Florence, Dr Andrew Hopkins; in London, Paul Agnew, Mike Albanese, Annabel Freyberg, Peter Fuller, Jonathan Hoyle, Robert Merrett, Thierry Muller, Yemi Osunkoya, Luis Peral-Aranda, Eduardo Viehra and Gareth Williams; in Los Angeles, my cousins Russ Jr and Ruthann Olsen, and Dr Volker Welter; in Milan, Francesco Fresca and the couturier Massimo; in New York, James Benjamin, and Benjamin and Cynthia Kracdur; in Paris, Basile and Paola Baudez; and in Winnipeg, Neil Einarson and Ryan Richard.

For especial help with procuring information and images, I am indebted to Simon Abbott, Nazli Arad, Maria Balfour, Henricke Becker, Wayne Berkowitz, Antonella Boisi, Dorthee Boissier, Ema Bonifacic, Sabrina Bosenberg, Emmanuel Brelot, Beverley Cable, Sean Campbell, Martina Caneparo, Teresa Charles, Rebecca Cheng, Valeria Czerny, Roxane Danset, Kevin Davis, Massimo de Conti, Mercedes de Rosas, Daymone Edmonds, Sarah Emburey, Federica Ernst, Tami Eyal, Serena Fong, Pascale Gibon, Jan Hamling, Melissa Johnston, Naihala Lasharie, Lauren Liorizzo, Paola Locati, Thomas Madory, Jonathan Makepeace, Karen Malacarne, Sylvie de Marne, Marieke Mars, Cristina Muller, Jelka Music, Claudio Occoffer, Cecilia Olive, Federica Otto, Pippa Patterson, Marilyn Porlan, Giorgio Re, Sandrine Reboux, Caroline Roux, Claire Sentis, Gideon Fink Shapiro, Eriko Shimazaki, Noona Smith-Peterson, Richard Sorger, Harriet Spence, Emi Sugiyama, Marie Le Tallec, Su Tan, Lucy Tasca, Janine Taylor, Joe Thiel, Dieter Tretter, Douglas Tuck, Siouxsie Webster, Danica Willi and Esther Zumsteg.

It would have been impossible to write the entries and introduction, especially the historical section, without the assistance of the knowledgeable librarians of the London College of Fashion, the London Metropolitan University (City), and particularly my former colleagues at the Royal Institute of British Architects.

Finally, I would like to thank Richard Sorger for casting his expert fashion eye over my text. And Jill Lever who, with the usual academic thoroughness and love of architecture she displayed when she was my chief curator of the RIBA Drawings Collection, made extremely helpful comments on my manuscript. However, I need hardly say, any mismatched socks in the book are mine.

Neil Bingham

INDEX